A Book of

Re-Membering

ISBN 978-0-578-01009-0

www.ABookofRemembering.com

An Introduction

Consciousness is birthed into form, with a veil of forgetfulness forming a barrier to the memory of time before. The blind embark on a journey with uncertainty. Challenges confront. The way is lost. Or so it appears. But Spirit is in control – though truth has been labeled myth and theory labeled fact, though we have been stripped of knowledge and have been fooled by the false prophets of belief – everything is as it should be.

Collectively we are learning. Even in our fallen and dismembered state, delusion gifts the lesson of discontentment. Ever, the seed that gestates within seeks union. An awakening is at hand. Slowly one begins to recall that which they already are. Clues emerge and gradually cross-correlate with one another to present a larger picture. Pieces are put together through diligent seeking; the unexplainable rushes in. Synchronicity laughs in our face. Knowledge kicks down the door.

This journal is the account of my own remembering, a process in which the familiar world around me crumbled, revealing something so complex and so seemingly chaotic that at times I was convinced I had lost my mind. In truth, I was simply regaining it.

A Book of Fear

[part one]

9.8.07: AND SO IT BEGINS

I have come down here to the jungles of Peru to do a ten-day dieta with ayahuasca in an effort to learn and heal. A primary intent that I set was to confront fear. Ironically, I have come armed and ready with four different types of mosquito repellant. How did this escape my attention?

The medicine was strong last night – really strong. At a certain point in the ceremony, I had to urinate so badly that I was compelled to do so in a way that seemed outside my conscious control. This was not an easy task, however; drunk on ayahuasca, stumbling in the pitch-black darkness toward what I thought was the general direction of the doorway. Though I was completely disoriented, I managed to find my way outside.

I stood at the entranceway of the Malorca and found that I could see even less with the flashlight on than with it off. The air was thicker than matter. All about me were swirling energies, patterns, and entities. I stood unsure of what to do, thinking perhaps I should let the current wave of vision that was upon me subside. After about a minute, I sat down in the dirt outside the entrance of the Malorca, as I was incapable of finding my way over to the bushes. Taking a leak would have to wait a little while, until I was better oriented within the remnants of reality.

The shaman was telepathically aware of where I was and what I was doing. I could feel Don J energetically reaching out to comfort me as he sang his holy song. After he finished his first icaro, he immediately began another, this time a more up-tempo and jovial one. I relaxed to the happy tune and began to find my center as I sat in the dirt mesmerized.

Unbeknownst to me, ants were crawling over my feet and legs, stationing themselves. All at once they attacked. My body lit up with sharp pain, as my mind instantly fell prey to confusion. I had no idea what was happening. It felt like I was being attacked by scorpions, and in my state of not knowing, I felt tremendous panic concerning poisonous insects.

The maestro changed his verse to "ha ha ha" and I could hear him laughing as he sang. The humor was lost on me.

STRANGE

The first time I drank ayahuasca a few years ago, I was shooting into outer space thinking, "Oh, this – of course." It was quite odd being familiar with such a unique altered state, having never experienced it previously. Last night I had another one of these déjà vu moments. At one point in the ceremony, I had a clear remembrance that I had made an agreement with the spirit of ayahuasca to work with her. It is quite odd how such an important thing could be hidden within the dark corridors of my brain, completely inaccessible in a normal state of awareness.

Strangely, the agreement seems like it was not made in this physical incarnation. It is difficult to explain or describe, or even to fully comprehend what this is all about. It is quite apparent to me that I have made a pact, yet I am at a loss to locate the specific memory within my mind of when.

9.10.07: SECOND CEREMONY

The ceremony last night presented wisdom so elegant in its simplicity, yet so inaccessible to an ordinary way of thinking – even now it fades from me. How unfortunate this seems! I wish I could remain in a heightened state of awareness and have everything remain that clear all of the time.

9.11.07: THE MEDICINE TAKES ROOT

I woke up this morning and cried. The amount of processing that I am doing is enormous. I probably got only about an hour of sleep last night. My brain was buzzing on overdrive until sunrise, trying to figure out what was occurring as my whole reality crumbled, bit by bit.

My mind is functioning in a way it hasn't before. Thought patterns are different. The amount of dislodged junk cluttering up my neural pathways is astounding. I am swimming in the shit of my own thoughts.

PLANT DIET

The secondary plant that I am taking on the dieta is called *bobinsana*. I drink about a quart of tea containing it every day. Bobinsana is a bush that grows on the banks of the river here in the Amazon. During the rainy season it becomes completely submerged under water, and during the dry season it may be many yards up above the waterline. It survives by tremendously long roots that penetrate deep into the earth. Physically, it lives within two different realities: those of both the wet and the dry season. The psychological effects of bobinsana within a human are harmonious with its physical attributes. It comfortably exists within dual realities of the dream state and the waking state, the wet and dry realms of consciousness. It is a bridge between these worlds.

I have been told simply that bobinsana helps with dreaming. But as much as it assists the dream to become lucid and awake, it has taken my waking hours and made them very dream-like. The whole dieta is turning into one long ceremony. The differences between being asleep or awake, sober or high on ayahuasca are all dissolving. Layers upon layers of lessons are forming a larger and amazingly orchestrated curriculum personally tailored for me.

DARK PONDERINGS

I had a literal vision of hell last night. I don't know where to place this vision, how to interpret it, or even how to comprehend it. I will just sit with it, as I have no other alternative. It shook me to the core.

9.12.07: GRASSHOPPERS & STAR BEINGS

Last night I was lying in my hammock when I saw this sort of insect-like geometrical image flash in my brain. It was like viewing something exoskeletol through a kaleidoscope. Thirty seconds later a large brown grasshopper showed up. Somehow I was not surprised; it seemed that on some level I was expecting him. Is there some kind of communication being introduced?

He slept on top of my mosquito net last night and has been hanging out with me all day, sitting on my backpack just a few feet from where I am writing. The grasshopper's body is about four inches long, and he has incredibly long antennas, which are an astounding twelve inches in length. We have become friends.

I've been observing the grasshopper, especially the way the long antennas are constantly vibrating as they send and receive information. Even in the stillness and quietness of the day, the grasshopper is picking up vibrations from distant noise within the jungle.

Earlier today I began making little clicking noises with my tongue while attempting to send thought-forms to this curious little being. He seemed to like this, and became very alert with his long thin receivers vibrating at a furious pace whenever I did so.

I had a vision of star beings last night. During my interaction with the grasshopper, my reflection upon them took a curious direction. Many indigenous cultures believe that our ancestors are from the stars, that they are waiting for us to grow up so that we may join them in their council. If this is the case, it makes sense that these beings have chosen a passive role in our evolutional development, allowing free will on the part of humanity. How else could we learn but by mistakes?

The thing about star beings I have been questioning is their level of advancement. Are those that may be our ancestors multi-dimensional? If so, then it stands to reason that they have an intimate understanding of matter. If I can have low-level communication with an insect, then it is most probable that they can do the same, though at a much higher level. This would hold true also with plants and animals.

While an insect might be having its own unique bodily experience, the collective consciousness of the species gains awareness through all individuals that comprise it. If an advanced star being of higher dimension is able to communicate with the collective spirit of an insect, animal, or bird, then it stands to reason that they would also have a pretty good pulse on the planet earth as a whole, both from an external and inherently internal perspective. The plant and animal kingdoms would serve as a sort of organic technology through their cooperation, working with higher beings to monitor and assist humanity in reaching a balanced state.

Cultures the world over have a history of working with animal spirits. Through my own experiences with many animal totems, I can validate that there is something very real about the whole shamanic worldview. If star beings do indeed have a vested interest in humanity or earth, it seems likely that they are likewise working with various totem spirits and consciousness collectives.

11

Back to my grasshopper friend: I have a deep feeling that I am being watched by a strong presence that has vast intelligence. 'Deep' is an understatement, in fact. The presence feels almost overwhelming at times.

EXPERIENCING CREATION

During ceremony last night, part of my awareness left my body. It shot out through space and time. I found myself existing as an orb of pure light... one among many. We came from the stars and descended upon the earth. We each impregnated Gaia with our being to bring about the birth of our souls within this planet's karmic cycle.

An orgy of light-energy making love with the spirit of the earth, it was an event of such brilliance that it is beyond my capability to describe. The feeling of union has been burned into my heart. I melt at the thought of it. It was the most beautiful thing I have ever experienced.

So stand my current reflections on the nature of star beings, and our relationship to them.

9.13.07: SHADOW BEINGS

Last night was one of the rest periods where we did not drink ayahuasca. For me, there was no rest. There was no sleep, only more processing. So many things are coming up. It seems I am recapitulating my whole life.

I discovered a couple of days ago just how fragmented my brain is. It is like Swiss cheese. I am as sane as I have ever been – more so in all likelihood – yet now I am realizing that I am completely neurotic and could be possibly schizophrenic. I really don't know. But if I were in fact crazy, how could I?

Though my thought process seems rational, I accept that I am completely nuts and actively battling deception. Most pressing within my mind at the moment is the fact that I have been having some intense bouts with demonic entities, battling nonstop. Even now the pretender voices rage.

I have known for many years that I am afflicted by these dark entities, and have had countless struggles against them in which they have become somewhat familiar. This battle is very intense and has been going on for days. I am being tricked at every moment. They are attempting to play me, creating an incredible confusion in my mind. Processing is difficult for me. There is nothing casual about thinking right now. I am kicking away doubt, fear, and shame at every corner. The pretender is loud. Be silent!

9.14.07: NON-LINEAR REALITY

There is no difference at this point between sleeping and dreaming. I've pretty much been time-traveling nonstop for the last couple of days. Actually, this isn't a very accurate description. Rather, part of my awareness is here in normal, waking reality, and part of it is in this non-linear place, jumping all around. I am cognitive of two different realities – sometimes more – at once. Even this very moment, sitting in my hut is nothing more than a dream.

It seems to be like a chess game, though with its own set of rules. The reality comprises a virtual labyrinth of possibilities, infinitely dangling like long rubber bands. Any input causes repercussions that cause other repercussions. Past, present, and future all occurring at once – and it is more interactive than I can fully comprehend. Time is different than I had understood.

The central theme in this journey consists of finding myself pulled into future apocalyptic scenarios in which I am killed. Then I am sucked into a new reality where I navigate the minefield of attacks a little better than before, again getting killed. Even now I have a split awareness of a dark, future timeline that I am methodically engaged within as I write.

I acknowledge that everything I am experiencing is based upon fear. I am engaged in some sort of spiritual warfare. Everything is so real and believable. I tell myself that I am experiencing a lie. I know this to be the case. Yet I cannot escape the feeling that in some sense these realities are preparing me for something. I seem compelled to engage them.

HELL

The vision I had three days ago in an ayahuasca ceremony was what commenced these dark dream states. It was extremely intense. The experience was this: I was standing on a knoll of a small hill as I watched multiple alien werewolf-like creatures galloping up towards me. They leapt through the air, flying at me. Initially I felt incredible fear, but this soon gave way to amazement. I watched and felt my arms swiping through the air, batting these monstrously large beasts away as if they were flies. I was not human, but instead something cat-like. I was huge and terrible.

The battle went on for a couple of minutes until I became overwhelmed by the number of beasts coming at me, and could not counter all their attacks. I was alone. The waves of attacks were unceasing.

It was then that I was overpowered and my body was torn apart. As my soul consciousness separated from the physical, darkness was all about. A great shadow beast devoured my awareness. Within its belly, the light-body of my soul developed a protective outer shell that encompassed it to form a solidified cyst-like state of my being. Paralyzed and powerless, I found myself a prisoner. Existing in a constant state of agitation, my misery fueled that which darkness fed upon. I had become a permanent energy source.

This is all so unpleasant. Is it hell? Am I to take this literally? Has this actually happened to me, or will it actually happen to me at some point in the future? My entire body trembles. I can feel my heart beating in my throat. Gulp.

SERPENTS & VIPERS

Ayahuasca is in union with God. She is a beautiful serpent spirit of our planet. She has an infinite energy source through her divine connection to the earth, universe, and all of creation. She is old and wise. She looks to humanity with compassion and seeks to assist us for our benefit as well as her own ensured future safety.

But the beast is an octopus-like creature. It is a viper with infinite tentacles and mouths to devour with. The beast has been disembodied and separated from its connection with the universe. It has no energy source of its own. It looks to humanity as its food source.

9.15.07: BREAKING CHAINS

I am nothing. I am everything. I am free.

The shadow beings have departed. I have a premonition that they will come back – imperceptibly, no doubt, for they excel at not being noticed. Their very survival depends upon it.

Likely I have been afflicted by shadow beings since childhood. It was at that time my family became involved in the Christian church. It was also then that I accepted guilt and shame into my life. Inevitably, such negative emotion attracts that which feeds upon it. As a teenager, my mother was heavily involved in bringing people out of the satanic church, and our home often served as a halfway house for members wishing to extricate themselves. Not all were sincere. There were multiple curses put upon my family. At one point we found a crucified crow hanging upside down under the house.

At twenty years old, I began experimenting with the psychedelic mushrooms. It was at that time that I began to see shadow beings. The first time this happened, I had eaten a lot of mushrooms one night while I was alone. The room began to change, and everywhere I looked I could see evil little beings comprising the whole fabric of perceived reality. There were thousands of miniscule faces in the carpet texture, on the wall, and on the ceiling. They were everywhere.

With my eyes closed it was even more disturbing. A dark entity extended its presence within my mind's eye, passing over and through my vision, going on and on. Its form was ever changing; it seemed to me as pure evil. I could feel sensation all over my body, like hundreds of spiders crawling over me. I thrashed about the room screaming and brushing myself off.

I ended up curled in a ball, powerless to cast them away or even pray for protection. Humorously, I could not remember the name of 'Jesus.' Even the word 'God' had been removed from my vocabulary. So there I lay curled up in a ball murmuring, "Help.

Please, help," hoping that the Divine One would hear me, and delivery me to safety.

9.16.07: REALITY CHECK

Today we broke the dieta. Don J said yesterday in the closing circle that many times the participant of an ayahuasca ceremony will experience incredible things, and feel that they are very powerful and very important. One should realize that a primary teaching method of ayahuasca is to show a person his or her own ego.

I am fairly certain that while told to the group, this advice was aimed specifically at me. I've been feeling pretty important the last week. It seems as if I am a pivotal character in the war of good against evil. I imagine myself as someone of great importance who is yet to come into his power. What does this say of my ego? Can I interpret everything I have experienced as literal events? Or were they simply custom-tailored realities derived from my own psyche that are relevant only to the process of learning? Was I even fighting anything outside of myself?

At this point it is dangerous to categorize anything. I have no basis upon which to accurately weigh or gauge things. I must keep all my lessons fluid and believe nothing. Experiences could be real. Or they could simply be lessons. I must be on guard against constructing a new worldview. Perhaps the correct task is to deconstruct my current one.

9.22.07: Sitting at Sacsayhuaman

I spoke to a Quechan man for about an hour here at this megalithic ancient ruin. He shared all sorts of things about Incan sites, history, and the current politics that natives are enduring. Sitting here amongst walls comprised of 100-ton boulders that are shaped and placed together like a jigsaw puzzle is quite amazing. The site gives cause to wonder. It is quite conducive to my current state of thoughtfulness.

The last day that I was in the jungle, I spoke at length to a friend who had some important words to share with me. His term for what I might find useful to reflect upon is 'objectification.' It is the process of assigning meanings and defining things to help us make sense of this thing called life. It is similar to adopting beliefs or worldviews, though less rigid, and done so with the understanding that the definition is not the be-all, end-all. Instead, it is a temporal lens to view things through until a bigger and better lens comes along to replace it.

I have punched a hole in the illusion of reality, and have no basis of categorization for anything. Without being able to categorize things, I cannot form any belief system or really even make logical sense. In some ways this may be a good thing, but it has left me in an immense state of confusion. The world around me presents only questions and offers no answers. I don't even have a reference point to begin from. Perhaps creating an objectified understanding of reality that is fluid and easily changeable will be good for me. Really, it is the only option that I seem to have.

Another thing my friend mentioned – actually he repeated himself three times until he could see a glint of understanding in my eyes – was this: One is not ready to take down the illusion until one feels no need to do so. By the term 'illusion,' I am referring here to the ordinary perception of reality.

It is ironic to receive his wise advice after the fact. I took quite a different path, diving in head first into the unknown without restraint. I repeatedly smashed my foundational reality with a sledgehammer, until I had nothing to stand upon. Perhaps this was foolish. Still, I must trust in some sort of divine plan in my life, and make the assumption that I have done things the correct way for myself. Obviously there will be more pieces to pick up with this method.

Now that I am back in the mundane world, things are different in a subtle way. I have a greater acceptance of how things are. As much as everything seems illusory, it is at the same time very real. Though this may seem like a conflicting viewpoint, my suspicion is that it is simply a paradox that I don't yet understand. There is a certain complexity and multidimensionality to the world that evades easy categorization. How is it that the infinite can mold itself into a dualistically viewed reality? Perhaps it is simply okay that nothing makes sense.

THE DAY I ALMOST SAW AN ANGEL

During one of the ayahuasca ceremonies, I relived an old memory with a bit of extra insight that I did not have during the original experience. I have been thinking about it a lot lately, as my re-experience of this event, along with some other encounters, have given rise to new questions about human nature.

Late one night I was in a park with my girlfriend at the time, and we were quite high on mushrooms. After walking for a while, we sat down on a bench in a section of the park that was unlit. As the moon was approaching fullness and there was a clearing in the trees around us, it was a pleasant spot to rest.

We had been sitting only a few moments when my heart went cold. I could feel the tension throughout my body. In front of us and to the right, there was an incredibly dark form about thirty feet away in the bushes. Because the bushes were shaded from the moonlight, they were black without discernable detail. However, there was a certain 'television static' quality about the blackness, wherein a great deal of dancing light could be observed. The shadow form, however, was blacker than black, devoid of all light. It was about six feet tall and was watching us closely. I felt complete emptiness in its presence.

I silently prayed for protection. I decided against getting up or doing anything to create vulnerability. I just sat there and monitored it. I acted completely normal and engaged my girlfriend with light-hearted small talk. This went on for a while.

Gradually, my feeling of uneasiness began to give way to relaxation, as I felt more and more confident of external protection from angels. At one point I became so comfortable that I forgot about the entity for a few seconds. When my attention was quite suddenly brought back to the shadow form, there was nothing there. At this point, we got up and strolled down through the park.

When we reached a lit section of the park, my partner asked me if I had seen anything at the bench. I confirmed that I had and asked her what she observed. In detail she described exactly what I had seen, though she had witnessed more than I. She described a point where the shadow form had charged towards us. Within a fraction of a second it was only a few feet from me when a white light came from behind me and rushed to intercept it. Then both light and darkness were gone instantly.

During a ceremony I relived this memory in detail. It very much seemed that it was not an outside entity that saved me, but rather an aspect of myself. It could have been just a transferred perspective of awareness I experienced. But I question whether there is a part of our higher self that is capable of splitting off and doing battle on the body's behalf.

Concepts such as an energetic double are acknowledged in shamanic circles. What of guardian angels? Are they external beings, or are they actually an aspect of the self? Are guardian angels different than doubles? Are they different from other angels? Or is it just different terminology between different knowledge schools, in which case we are actually our own guardians? I am completely confused about these matters.

MOTHS & RAVENS

Last week a moth found its way inside my mosquito netting while I was going to sleep. It landed on my toe, and felt quite ticklish. I jumped and it flew away. I put forth a lame effort to get it out of my netting, but soon gave up because I was so tired. Gradually I acquiesced to it, allowing the moth to walk around on my body. At one point, it fluttered into my ear, which was quite unnerving. And then it was gone.

Soon after, a subtle sound of flapping wings encircled my hut and got louder and louder until it seemed to be all about. The pace of movement and quality of sound led me to believe that it was something with enormous wings. Whatever was creating this motion, I soon realized, was inside my mosquito net and literally right above me.

I could feel air stirring up against my face. I lay frozen, with my eyes wide open, trying to discern what was about me. As though a veil gradually dissolved, I first began to see movement of a form, and then the slightest of detail within the darkness about me. I stared, certain that I was observing a large raven around 5 feet tall, standing over me.

Initially I was quite alarmed. Though, the soothing pace of its wing movement gradually comforted me until all fear left. I had a vague notion of who or what it might be. Then it disappeared. I dozed off.

A short while later I awoke from my sleep to again find that there was something within my mosquito net, standing over me. This time it seemed to have more human qualities.

Over the next few hours it hunted physical parasites within me – things I had been trying to rid myself of for years. It felt like the being had a string attached to a little piece of wood that was lying on my abdomen. The piece of wood would slowly move around scanning, until it found a parasite. At this point I could feel the located worm flopping about inside me, as a tremendous jolt of electricity went through the stringed apparatus and into my body for about fifteen seconds. All movement and life departed the parasite. All my muscles in the area knotted involuntarily during the bursts of energy. It was quite painful. Then scanning would commence in search of the next. It seemed very much like fishing.

After an hour of this I had to urinate so badly that I could no longer hold it. I reached up to brush the line and wood apparatus off me as I got up, but there was nothing there. Nobody was in my tambo except me. I was surprised.

After taking a leak, I climbed back into bed. Immediately I heard creaking in the floorboards as something walked across my tambo, and then right through the mosquito net to begin the process again. I was surprised that something without physical form could have a discernable weight.

The next morning the entire region from my inner thighs to my upper stomach was extremely sore. I had some doubts to the whole experience, as it occurred a couple hours after a ceremony, and I was still a little high. Upon defecating, I noticed that my feces were filled with dead flukes. I went so far as to poke things around with a stick, examining thoroughly.

While part of me is at a loss to find a logical explanation of the whole experience, I am quite certain that I did not imagine this. This particular visit left concrete evidence that I was experiencing something other than a lucid dream-state hallucination.

There were other visits; each time the being stayed for hours while it patiently and methodically manipulated various things. There was one night that it began peeling my energy body away from that of my physical body. It was a slow process that began by lifting my energetic fingertips millimeter by millimeter, then my hands. Then toes and feet were peeled apart; then arms, legs, hips, and torso as well. In the end, only my neck and head were bound together. I had dual sensation and could tangibly feel my separated energy body along with my physical one. I could move the energetic body with great effort, but mostly it seemed lethargic and in a somewhat paralyzed state. Wiggling a second set of fingers was definitely a trip.

That was the night that I started thinking a lot about things like the double, shape shifting, and angels. I haven't stopped.

THE ENERGY BODY

Carlos Casteneda gave a mysterious yet eloquent description of the energy body in his writings. He described it as a 'luminous cocoon,' which is an egg-shaped energetic vortex that surrounds a person. It serves many purposes, and is as much a part of the person as the physical body. During his early apprenticeship to Don Juan, Carlos could not actually see the luminous cocoon. Instead he would ask a tremendous amount of questions to his teacher, who would then relay elaborate descriptions of the energy body. On and on Casteneda would write these second-hand descriptions until one day after much personal work, he was able to see the energy body for himself.

When he was finally able to see the luminous cocoons of people around him, Casteneda became lightheaded and nauseous. Don Juan looked on, rolling over with laughter. What Carlos saw fell far short of his expectations. He witnessed distorted monstrosities. The luminous cocoons were all twisted and abnormally shaped. Some didn't even go past the knees. All were disturbing save one: Don Juan's, which was a perfectly egg-shaped luminous sphere.

MY ENERGY BODY

Years ago I apprenticed to a Nagual by the initials of SD. He was quite adept at reading the energy body, and had a very scientific process that resulted in about 7 pages of data. These consisted of a basic diagram along with actual measurements of the nine layers of the aura that comprise the luminous cocoon.

After studying with him for a year, he drew a diagram of my energy body. It was not a pretty site. Though my luminous cocoon extended to my feet, it was twisted, and in sort of a 'C' shape, where it curved in a concave manner towards the right side of my abdomen.

It was then that SD told me of shadow beings and how they feed off the energy of humans. Within the diagram, it was illustrated how I had been fed upon. Additionally, I could view how certain parts of my energy body had actually been reclaimed through my personal spiritual work and healing.

SD was quite matter-of-fact in his view that almost all humans are fed upon by shadow beings. In order to eradicate a shadow being from one's life, the primary step is to guard one's thoughts and emotions from negativity in order to gradually starve them. As the energy vibration of the host becomes lacking in sufficient negative quality, the shadows will begin to periodically leave in order to find other sustenance. Over time, a person reclaiming their wholeness becomes a poorly inhabitable host... and should eventually take a stand to either permanently banish or kill their shadow beings.

I believe this to be the case. Through my little battles I am receiving more and more confirmation that this is really occurring.

THOUGHTS ON SHADOW BEINGS

As shadow beings are not physical entities, it seems self-evident that their primary dimension of inhabitation is not the third. They have a different relationship to time than the physical does. They seem to not only know the past and future, but be actively engaged in a simultaneous experience of past, present and future in each moment. Shadow beings also seem to be part of a larger organism. Though they have individuality, they seem to share a common mind. When one learns something, they all know it.

I am trying to keep openness in observing and assessing their nature, and find myself prefacing thoughts with terms like "seems to be." But the truth is that I find myself simply knowing a great deal about them. During the ayahuasca experience where I went to hell within the belly of a shadow being, I received a tremendous 'download' regarding their nature. As I was held prisoner, their victory was short-lived. Both the entity that had captured me and myself realized that I was now possessing it, living within its being, and gleaning information concerning its nature. I was spit out fairly quickly after this realization.

I find myself quite certain of interesting little tidbits of information about them that I just seem to know. I am disturbed by the overall picture of their plan – it is thoroughly coordinated and brilliant. Beyond the mental, emotional, physical, spiritual, and sexual slavery of mankind – things already achieved – there is something more nefarious at hand.

Perhaps it is better not to indulge what I think I know about them. I must err on the side of caution. It is both possible and probable that the shadow being played an active role in downloading me with information about these matters, and if this were the case, that information could of course not be trusted. Likely their power and influence were overstated in an effort to seed a growing fear within me. Honestly, I do feel much more trepidation about them now than I had previously felt.

GOLD HORSE PROPHECY

The Hopi Indians have many prophecies relating to the times that we are currently living in. One of these seems quite relevant to all that I am pondering on spiritual warfare.

At the end of the great cycle of time, a race ensues between four horses. The first horse is black, and is the representation of darkness and human suffering. The second horse is red, and represents warfare. The third horse is white, representing technology. The fourth horse is gold. The gold horse is the light of humanity.

As the race begins, the black horse heads to the front of the pack, followed in second place by the red horse. The white horse holds a steady pace at third, while the gold horse begins to fall behind. The black horse feels the steady hoof-beats of the red horse behind him, and is fueled with increased strength. He steadily increases his lead. A symbiotic relationship begins to exist, where the white horse's speed propels the red horse, whose strength is in turn utilized by the black horse. Technology is harnessed to propagate war, causing suffering and destruction. The black horse's lead has become immense. All the while the gold horse is far behind.

The race begins to look hopeless to the light and loving side of humanity. The black horse is hungry for victory, and the race is nearing the end. Soon all hope is gone. But then something unexpected happens; even miraculous. The gold horse begins to pick up speed. Though slowly at first, he accelerates rapidly. The gold horse eases past the white horse. Then he storms past the red horse. The dark horse maintains a good lead as the finish line draws near. But the gold horse closes the distance between them. Soon it is upon the black horse and begins to pass. They are neck and neck as they approach the finish line.

The prophecy does not tell who won the race. Perhaps the outcome was withheld lest we either lose hope or become lazy in a sense of assuredness of victory. Or maybe it was unknown. With such an incredibly close outcome and the inherit complexities concerning the nature of time, my guess is that either outcome could occur. The decision is ours.

9.23.07: PLANTING A SEED

When Jesus said that a person could not enter the Kingdom of Heaven unless they were born again, what was his meaning? Obviously he was not saying that one must speak the later-concocted sinner's prayer to be saved as commonly accepted today. I contemplate that few have ever understood him.

Rather than a figurative metaphor, I question if he was speaking literally. Was he talking about a transformative rebirth of the energy body? Was he speaking of a reconfiguration of the luminous cocoon and some sort of awakening that accompanies such an event? Would the death of the old self be a prerequisite?

OMENS

What of these? I had an incredibly large condor fly by me in the jungle after the dieta. Was this bird simply going about its day, or was there a message contained for me within? The communication of signs and omens seems to be in a dynamic and fluid language where the medicine of an animal, its quality of movement, and my current life-state all come into play together with many other variables. Sometimes the message is immediately apparent. Sometimes it is not understood until time has passed, if even at all.

I was opened up to the concept of omens in a dramatic fashion. A couple years ago I had three owl appearances within a one-month span. The first appearance was at night while I was driving a backcountry road with my dog. An owl swooped down and filled the entire view from my windshield with its wings spread, as I slammed on the brakes. The air current surrounding my car carried it safely over me.

A couple of weeks later I was driving on the freeway during the day, when precisely the same thing occurred. This time I saw the owl a second before it descended upon me and swerved the car. The vehicle behind me hit it head on with a flurry of feathers scattering about.

With the third appearance, I was the front seat passenger in a van with some friends. Again, an owl swooped down. This time it was hit quite hard. We stopped the vehicle and got out. The owl was gone, nowhere to be seen.

Not surprisingly, the owl medicine that unfolded in my life soon after was intense.

10.01.07: FOUR HORSES

After spending several days in Machu Picchu, I have returned here to Cusco. Yesterday while perusing the town, I walked into a store and was surprised to find there a painting that depicted an Incan man stretched and torn apart at the hands of the conquistadors. Galloping across the sky were a white horse, a black horse, a red horse, and a gold horse. I spent many hours asking around and looking in the local library to find out if the indigenous people of Peru had a similar tale to that of the Hopi. I discovered nothing.

It seems more than odd to have just written about the Gold Horse Prophecy and then to have suddenly come across such a painting.

12.12.07: ISOLATION

The work, cleansing, and intent I put forth in the dieta have had an immediate impact on the structure of my daily life. After returning to the United States, I chose to discontinue any effort involved in maintaining 'normalcy' along with the vast amounts of energy required to hold my glass house together. I allowed my affairs to dissolve.

While escaping can be a misguided solution, I have been quite unhappy. It feels like the right thing to do. Presently I am living up in the woods, unemployed. My current state of life is beneficial to my process, as it allows me a great deal of time for reflection.

STEPPING THROUGH THE VEIL

A couple of nights ago I decided to drop seven hits of LSD and do some personal ceremony that consisted of invoking the Sacred Ones and singing to them. About an hour into things I became very sensitive. I could hear and feel a buzz of electricity circulating within the walls of my house. At a certain point I became aware of the smell of propane coming from my gas furnace. As these seemed only minor distractions, I continued with my songs and prayers. I told myself that my senses were just heightened.

Soon I realized that the scent was becoming stronger, and that I was laboring to breathe. I rationalized that I was only imagining this. I continued with the ceremony. My thoughts became very cloudy, and after a few more minutes I came to the sudden realization that I was actually suffocating. I could hardly breathe.

I got up and went outside. A surge of oxygen came into my lungs, and within a minute I regained clarity. I looked in the house and it was thick with haze. Indeed something was transpiring.

As it was very cold outside, I decided to drive down the mountain to town where I could sleep at a friend's place, which was about seven miles away. I went back in the house only to find that my keys were lost. I spent another ten minutes looking for them, every minute or two going outside for a few breaths of oxygen. Finally I found my keys and proceeded to my vehicle.

Upon stepping off the deck, a flurry of shadow beings that I could physically see descended upon me in an ambush, with light being intervention. I was too surprised to feel any fear. These beings had come close enough that they pierced my energy body and I had a sensation of air brushing against my face. It was quite unnerving.
In that moment I understood that I was engaged in a spiritual battle. But I didn't believe it. I had never experienced such an attack, where the veil was thin enough that entities could step through and have a direct influence within the physical realm. Confused, I argued with myself about the nature of what was occurring as I stumbled to the automobile.

All the doors were frozen shut. I persistently yanked on them as waves of shadow beings descended, regrouped, and again dove upon me. At this point I became frantic, and decided to take this all very seriously, regardless of what may or may not be happening.

After failing to open both front doors, I finally managed to open the rear passenger door. I got in and drove down the dirt road, with a herd of deer cutting in front of me. They ran in my path for a few seconds before leaving the road. There were seven of them.

My vehicle has full-time 4wd and extremely good traction. The trip to town is completely downhill, at an approximate 6% downgrade. Generally I use the gears to slow myself down so that I don't have to ride the brakes the whole time. Though flying down the mountain in fourth has never been a problem, on this particular night I couldn't get out of second gear without the tires spinning. I drove downhill with my foot on the gas pedal at 25 mph, my tires unable to keep traction at any greater speed.

As I drove, I watched continual waves of a green liquid coming up from the gravel shoulder to spread across my path. Dozens of times I found myself slipping sideways down the hill. I also watched as thousands of snake embodiments slid their way in front of me and under my tires. I came to understand that they were giving my tires traction.

I had never experienced anything like this. I was having a complete Ayahuasca vision manifest in physical reality. I could have written the whole thing off as a bad trip, were it not for the fact that I was driving downhill with enough resistance that I could barely make progress. It was completely illogical. I could not accept what was happening, and yet could not deny physical evidence such as the vehicle laboring to go downhill. It was a defiance of gravity.

So I took everything seriously. I prayed and sang as I drove. I used tone to resonate throughout my body. I called powers. I rebuked fear and anger. Anything that came to mind, I did without hesitation, and did whole-heartedly.

For example, when I thought about lightening my vibration and releasing the fear I was feeling, I stuck a finger down my throat and vomited in my lap and on my new poncho. I became upset at this point about my poncho being soiled, which set me on my next task of releasing attachments to physical possessions. Soon my poncho was torn, my necklace was in pieces, and my wallet and cell phone were flying out the window.

When I got to the bottom of the hill, I pulled over to make my stand in a field. I could drive no further. I quickly removed my clothing and ran butt-naked into the field, where I laid in the frosty grass. I was compelled to be as vulnerable as possible. It was probably around midnight, and about twenty degrees outside.

On my back I observed a battle that was taking place in the sky above me, with thousands of entities involved. Black shadows swarmed in waves. A lighter, more formless mist repelled them. There was no safety or comfort that I felt. Darkness appeared to have the upper hand, and there were a great many more of the dark beings. As I observed the war about me, I had the clear realization that the outcome of this battle was dependent upon me.

I sang and prayed at the top of my lungs. When the shadows were able to many times pierce through defensive angelic lines and make contact with me, I found myself suddenly a 13th degree black belt with ten claws swiping through the air to bat them away. In the next moment as they regrouped, I would switch into a feminine and passive state with an open-heart space singing of love, gratitude, and forgiveness. This went on and on.

After about 20 minutes, I was exhausted and my extremities were so cold that I could not move my fingers. My voice was horse. My lungs labored. My physical body had nothing left to resist with. Still the battle raged.

The outcome appeared bleak at this point. I noticed eerie similarities between what I was experiencing and my previous vision of battling were-beasts. I thought of the dark ayahuasca vision and wondered if it foretold of this event. Was my body to die? Was my soul consciousness to be devoured by shadow beings and imprisoned within? I began to lose hope.

Shadows surrounded me. I gave thanks to Great Spirit as I prepared for death. I thought of Christ and the price he paid. I lay there feeling a great sadness, but no regret. I wondered if the man Jesus knew that he would resurrect, or did he pay the ultimate sacrifice by giving himself unconditionally, not knowing that he would be victorious in the end? I marveled at the lengths love would go to for another. I thought of my family and what lengths I would be willing to go to for them. It was then that I understood forgiveness for the first time. I stopped fighting.

My vision became darker and darker. Soon I could only see black.

Then stillness came. Black turned to purple, then violet, then white. Then it dissipated to reveal the starry night about me. I could see continued movement in the distance as the shadows were chased off. I became aware of how cold my body was, and made my way back to the vehicle. I was completely sober at this point.

As much as I would like to write this off as a fantastic hallucination, the next day upon returning home revealed that my big propane tank was completely empty. It had recently been filled in preparation for winter.

12.23.07: WORDS

I had a very simple realization today: English is not God's native tongue. I have been personifying Great Spirit in my mind, trying to differentiate the various voices in my head so that I can distinguish that which is His.

A continual stream of vibration surrounds and penetrates my being. This is the dialog God has with me. Should my conscious mind occasionally translate love-energy into thought, into word-form, and should I relay a message to myself by speaking to myself, this would indeed be good. Though, it would still merely be me talking to myself. To reach beneath the mind and penetrate beyond it, to merge my awareness with the vibration of creation: this interests me more.

Must I lose my mind if I am to truly understand the spiritual dialog that is taking place within and around me? How do I release the ego's grip of control? I wish to remove restrictions that filter out the nonstop dialog occurring with the Source.

TRAVELING IN TIME

Recently my parents, on a whim, decided to go visit my sister and their grandchildren. One day while everyone was gone from the house except my father and ten-year-old niece, a near tragedy was averted.

My niece, who is an excellent swimmer, was playing in the pool unsupervised as she always does. She began having a little fun with the automatic vacuuming robot that wandered about the pool. The vacuum proceeded to suck her hair into it, and she began screaming.

My father ran out of the house and jumped in the pool as my niece dogpaddled, barely able to keep her nose above the water. He couldn't pull her hair out. The suction was too strong. He swam over to disconnect the vacuum hose at the intake filter, and the ordeal was soon over.

One could view this as random luck in good timing, or as a greater power directing one's steps so that they are in the right place at the right time. I think the relationship that our higher self has to time is more intricate and deeper than most fathom. We are not separate from the greater power. We are cooperating as we engage in co-creating our reality.

From my perspective, we're all time traveling, and likely unconsciously directing our own steps to a great degree. If the soul does not exist within the matter confines of the 3rd dimension, how could we not have an aspect of the self that is unbound by the limitations of time?

MEDITATION ON BEING HUMAN

The friend who told me after my dieta that I should meditate on 'objectification' has proven to be quite a blessing in my growth. He humorously has the habit of giving me synchronistic advice that is the exact opposite of what I have just done. Obviously this challenges me to examine all assumptions.

Following a ceremony last month, we were checking in with one another about our experiences, and he said something that surprised me. He had been doing a meditation on what it means to be human. Simply being human – nothing more and nothing less.

Perhaps I am getting a little too far out with my ponderings on star being heritage and God-union birthright. I am a human; I admit this. I just don't know exactly what a human is.

1.30.08: ANOTHER NOT-FUN TRIP

A couple of nights ago I had another intense spiritual battle during personal ceremony. It seems that I've come to the place where the veil is really thin for me when I enter an altered state. While previous to the dieta I could do this without vulnerability, now I am now becoming increasingly responsible for my own protection. Spiritual entities are able to step through to the physical, where they can tangibly engage with me. Or maybe it is I who step through to the nonphysical, giving them a bridge to this realm.

When the attack began, a thought instantly arose in my mind of an agreement I had made with myself last fall while on the medicine, which I have since broken. It seemed to me as if I had created a doorway through my decisions and actions. Indiscretion literally gave permission for shadow beings to antagonize me.

Atonement was required. Forgiveness was required. An offering was required. All were given. This attack was diffused very quickly and not nearly as dramatic as the last one. Regardless, I am going to slow down on these personal escapades for a bit.

1.31.08: ATONEMENT

Last spring I purchased a shovel, which I have never used. Over the last few weeks I have thought of this shovel a dozen times, as I am downsizing my life in preparation for travel. I didn't know what to do with it. I've almost taken it to Goodwill several times.

In an effort to get rid of all the clutter in my life, I've been going through old boxes and have come across many curious items: a mask I once made, an old bible, the collar of my deceased dog, a Sundance shield, rocks, feathers, and many other things. I likewise no longer wished to keep these. All of these things have ended up in a corner of my house, forming a 'figure out what to do with you later' pile.

On the night of my last personal ceremony, I received a phone call. I had called a friend earlier to have her pray on my behalf, and she called back to tell me that I needed to make gazpacho. I told her that she should make it for me, as I don't cook. She corrected me. I was to make 'despacho,' which is an offering where I bury things in the earth. I understood immediately. It was obvious why I had purchased a shovel and gone through boxes, pulling out the exact items required for giveaways to the earth mother. I stayed up all night and made my offering at first light.

AGREEMENTS

I've been soliciting some advice on what it means to break an agreement with oneself. The general consensus seems to be that it is okay to do this, for such agreements can always be renegotiated. Yet I cannot escape the thought of an entirely different perspective. It seems that any agreement we make is of utmost importance. Renegotiating the agreement is one thing, but breaking it is not good, especially if the agreement was made with ayahuasca. Energetic protection seems to be only as strong as one's integrity.

2.1.08: ACCESSING THE PSYCHE

At the height of my disoriented mind-state in the jungle I wrote a note to myself that I should get hypnotized; this statement was followed by several exclamation marks. I haven't known why. After procrastinating for months, I finally did it yesterday. The woman I worked with was more of a shaman taking me on a guided journey than a traditional hypnotist. She was very much in her power and aligned with Spirit.

She took me through to a past life, where I found myself in a land of symbol rather than a literal lifetime. Upon looking down, I noticed I was wearing sandals that were too big and on the wrong feet. I was holding a spear, and appeared to be a Roman soldier.

In front of me lay a tiger with a couple of arrows protruding from its ribcage. It seemed dead. Apparently I was the one who had slain him, and was feeling both sorrow and regret that such a beautiful animal had been brought down.

Suddenly the tiger rose to its feet and stood to look at me. I was directed to remove the arrows from his side, and upon doing so, found that the dark arrowheads were alive. They were black and moving. They were literally little shadow beings. I stuck the arrows into the earth.

All that my subconscious was communicating to me through this experience seemed very much in line with what my lessons have been showing me. The tiger is my power. I am the one responsible for my own wounding and disempowerment. It is time to step into my power.

2.11.08: DEMON SLAYER

Last summer I had an experience with a shadow being shortly before the dieta. A friend and I decided to go on a full moon hike and do a mushroom ceremony together. After a few hours of hiking along a ridge, amongst tall pines, we traversed up a bluff to where we could view the valley below for miles.

It was here on top of this little peak that we smoked DMT. Combined with an already psychedelically enhanced mind-state, this created an incredibly magnified experience that we refer to as 'launching.' Within a launch, the mushroom trip accelerates in intensity to that of an ayahuasca trip, but very much within the realm of psilocybin consciousness.

My friend was aware that I had been actively battling shadows, and set it in his mind to help me confront one. However, he did not inform me of this ahead of time. We sat down facing one another and set out to launch simultaneously. We agreed to test our telepathy and attempt to enter the same landscape.

As we sat there ready to go, I felt an incredible amount of fear and reservation. It was unusual. I began talking, stalling for extra time. I felt uneasy. Unable to pacify myself, I said, "Screw it," and we launched together.

Soon I was in a strange landscape with ancient temple structures that were filled with symbols. The world began to undulate and change, becoming fluid and alive. Structures became living entities that interacted with me. A beautiful creature reached its form through my mind's eye and beyond. Then the beauty began to dissipate, and I recognized that this was a shadow being. I examined the incredible detail of the entity.

At one point, a few minutes into the experience, the shadow being convulsed in such a quick and dramatic fashion that I started laughing. I could hear my friend laughing too. It was quite funny for some absurd reason. Perhaps it was just unexpected and out of character for this strong and regal entity to be recoiling in such a weak fashion. Once we began laughing, however, things got out of hand.

The shadow being began thrashing about dramatically, all the while growing smaller and smaller. Soon it was a tiny little creature convulsing in desperation. We continued laughing. Then all movement stopped. It had become a miniscule puddle that was absolutely motionless.

At that point I couldn't believe what had just happened, and opened my eyes. My friend startled me, as he was only a few inches from my face with a really big grin. Apparently he had been focusing incredible amounts of love on me during the launch.

After a few minutes, when I was finally able to stop an uncontrollable laughter, I relayed my experience to him: "Holy shit. Demons can be killed?" His response was simply that he knew.

2.13.08: SALVATION

Given my resistance to Christianity, it is quite something that I have recently asked Christ to come into my heart. Really, there was no other way for me. I had to seek resolution within myself.

My 'conversion' was unorthodox. It took place during the mushroom ceremony of my last attack, shortly before I made despacho. I didn't think about getting saved, and I didn't say the sinner's prayer. Rather, I meditated on forgiveness and compassion. Then I invited the Christ within.

The larger irony is that I was well aware that Christ was already a part of me. I had just raged so much against the Church and their deception, even to the point of becoming angry at the host-body of the Christ, the man called Jesus. Perhaps he needed my forgiveness as much as I needed his.

I don't know if anything changed. But I do feel a great deal of reconciliation on the matter. That is something.

2.21.08: CONSPIRACY THEORY

I've spent years researching revisionist history, such as the Sumerian stories of the Annunaki creating a genetic half-breed of star being and primitive man. This resulted in 'A-Dama,' which literally means 'the earthling.' This would be the biblical Adam, who experienced a separation. Upon receiving the gift of knowledge, he lost his ability to communicate with animals. He experienced separation, no longer at one with creation. Within the Sumarian clay tablature, the stories tell how human DNA was altered and locked, in an Annunaki effort to keep mankind from evolving to the point where they could usurp control from the 'gods.'

In the current day, any person up on their conspiracy theory would probably hold the opinion that an array of efforts by religious, financial, and government institutions are perpetrated by world controllers to keep humanity dumbed-down and manipulated.

Personally, I think it goes deeper than this. I question whether the face of the physical struggle between freedom and control within humanity is but a reflection of the deeper battle occurring within our genetics.

I am going through a metamorphosis. There are tangible things happening to my body and senses. For example, I can hear ringing harmonies in my ears, which I surmise is some sort of creation song unfolding. I am tuning into gifts that I have never possessed before, such as strong intuitions and even telepathy at times.

I am hesitant to buy into any New Age hype, but it very much feels like my DNA is evolving. In some sense, it feels like I am engaged in actually unlocking what has been previously bound.

3.15.08: EXORCISM

I did three ayahuasca ceremonies approximately a week ago. On the third ceremony, I lost it – completely. I experienced a time-split with part of my awareness in some future apocalyptic battle and the other part reliving my birth.

The birth was quite something. The experience entailed getting ambushed as my consciousness entered this world in a New

Orleans delivery room. I had complete awareness as a shadow being violated and then entered my energy body for the three-day duration that I was jaundiced before being baptized/given to God as an infant. His imprisonment within the coolness of my soul was his own bastardized version of Christ's descent into hell. His resurrection from my being after three days was yet the same.

As disturbing as this was to experience, I've known my whole life that something traumatic occurred at my birth, so I wasn't really too surprised. What shocked me and completely broke me down emotionally was the realization that this was done with my consent. I had agreed to the whole violation of my being from the onset of this incarnation. Why? I don't know.

By this point in the ceremony I had crawled to the bathroom and was quite disoriented. While part of my awareness was experiencing an induced and traumatic birthing at the hands of a possessed physician, another part of me was engaged in apocalyptic, hand-to-hand battle scenarios in the future. Actually, claw-to-claw is more accurate. These were so intense that the part of me curled over the toilet was barely conscious.

At this point I vomited up something very large. Even now I do not know what it was. I flushed the toilet, but it did not go down. As the water level of the clogged toilet crept up to the rim of the bowl, a dark entity circled about me, tormenting me. It surrounded me. When I forgave it, the shadow being went berserk and lashed out at me. I became confused and literally lost my mind.

I left the bathroom and caused a commotion before going outside where I tried to crawl into the earth. It took four people holding and shaking me to bring my mind back.

Something that had been with me a long time was gone.

A CRAZY WEEK

It has been seven days since the ayahuasca ceremonies. I have been unable to sleep and engaged in a state somewhere between reality and who-knows-what. Actually, being unable to sleep isn't completely accurate. Rather, every time I go to sleep I am sucked into dream realities that have dire physical consequences for me. It is only while I am awake that I have any perceived safety.

The last week I have been doing cleansing ceremonies all day and all night, pretty much non-stop. They have been intuitive and fluid, laying my life bare in the process. I burned my most prized possession of a painting I recently completed along with the original handwritten manuscript of this journal. I've disposed of all my books and most of my clothes. I've made two despacho offerings.

This has not been country club-esque spirituality. I am fighting for my life. Or so it appears. Though a deeper part of me keeps reminding myself that everything is okay, I am taking all perceptions at face value as an added precaution. Strangely, I had foreknowledge that this would occur. A random thought came into my mind as I was driving home that I would be engaged in spiritual warfare for seven days. I just didn't realize the severity that would unfold.

Having dream battles are one thing, but they seem to be linked to manifestations in the third dimension. For example, five days ago I began having sharp heart pains. The next day I did a thorough house cleaning. When I removed my bedspread, the comforter had a two-foot circle of blood on it right at the spot that covered my chest. There were many little slit holes within this area of the comforter, and feathers were everywhere within the comforter cover.

Later that day while dragging out various items to burn, I came across one of my kitchen knives, four feet off the back deck in my yard. It was bent in half, forming a 90-degree angle where the blade met the handle. The blade matched the size of the holes within my comforter exactly. Even now, many days later, I still have a persistent pain within the center of my chest.

Then there was observing my locked door slowly opening in the middle of the night, finding the ten-foot-tall rear property fence cut open from top to bottom, and on and on. There have been many other events in the physical world. Some are too unbelievable to write about.

SURRENDERING

I just took about a two-hour nap and am feeling much better. This is the first sleep I've had all week. I awoke with some clarity on time travel, only to be interrupted by the thought that the phone was going to ring. Five seconds later, it did.

Time is a lie. I've put in such an effort to understand the phenomenon that I have made the whole thing very logical in my mind, and even come to believe my theories. This is just plain ignorance. It is a bit like being a blind passenger in a moving car and theorizing on the nature of the route and qualities of the passing landscape.

MY STORY

What once served as a useful container of my world-view, animating my identity and providing a palatable purpose, has now become an obstacle. I can see beyond it. I am quite aware of the limitations that my story has set upon me. Beyond perceptions, there is a much larger story that is an incomprehensible stream of consciousness. It is with both sadness and joy that I say goodbye to the person who I once thought was I.

3.30.08: THE BUBBA CHRIST

Once I was a pet human to a dog. He was a lion and a lamb – a fifty-pound, yellow pit-bull/lab mix. I called him Leo. He came into my life to teach me about joy and suffering. He came to teach me about love through the unconditional giving of his energy, and ultimately his life.

I found Leo about fifteen miles up an old logging road in the forest when he was a puppy. On the ride home, Leo looked up at me with his big almond eyes and appeared very alien. I baby-talked him as he sat on my lap, joking that the celestial beings had come in their space ships and dropped him off in the woods. He informed me that I was right, though I didn't think I heard him correctly at the time.

We had a telepathic understanding. I rarely gave verbal commands, as a grunt was understood. Leo was extremely intelligent and sensitive to what it was that I wanted. As he grew and our connection evolved, I would experiment with this, and was continually surprised. If I was in the other room and even had a thought about going out for a walk, he would come running.

Leo was a lover. He was gentle and playful. I cuddled and coddled him, often like a baby. These are my fondest memories of him. He was so sweet that it was easy to forget he was a dominant male with big testicles. Of this I was reminded often.

Leo loved to fight. Since I never used a leash with him, he had ample opportunity. His interest lay only in attacking large alpha males that dwarfed him. Leo would latch onto their necks pretty quickly, and then do the typical head-shake. He would refuse to let go. After about two years of some pretty creative and useless techniques, I finally learned how to force a release. By the time he was five, he would release upon command.

When he was six, we were jumped in an alley by two unneutered male pit-bulls, which were each twice Leo's size. I was relatively safe in the middle of the fight, as it was my dog they were trying to kill. I got many kicks in, but spent more time in the dirt than actually helping him. The speed and circular movement of action was so fast that my high center of gravity made me useless.

In the firestorm of dust and blood that was spattering about, I was certain that Leo didn't stand a chance between two dogs, and was as good as dead. One lock on him was all that it would have taken – I have no doubt about it. But fear gave way to marvel, as Leo moved with such speed that it seemed he was defying physics. He continually evaded, circling around with a slash to a nose or tooth ripping through an ear.

After a couple of minutes – an excruciating period of time that seemed to never end – the owner of the pit-bulls finally came running out and called his dogs off. It was over. Leo did not have a scratch on him.

That was the last fight he was ever involved in. About three months later, I was at a coffee shop when I looked over to see Leo nose to nose with a massive wolf husky. The two had a mutual disdain for each other and had been itching to fight for a while, but never had the opportunity.

I began slowly walking over, knowing that any sudden movement would set things into action. When I was about twenty feet away, the wolf lunged. In reaction, Leo jumped up in the air to do a 180-degree body twist, hitting him in the side of the face with his muscular buttock.

I was shocked. I had never seen Leo pass up a fight with such a dominant male, nor humiliate one in such a comical way. The wolf lunged one more time, and Leo did the same thing, completely unthreatened, with an ear-to-ear grin. At that point, I kicked the dog in the head and threw Leo over my shoulder. I walked off laughing. Leo was king.

His other favorite thing was humping. We walked the streets and alleys at night. In the very rare occasion that a bitch in heat came across our paths, Leo had his way with her. I would stand there pretending to look the other way whenever someone walked by. Perhaps I could have been a more upstanding citizen, but I loved that dog more than life itself, and seeing him happy was my greatest joy.

One night we were driving together when an owl swooped in front of the car. In this very moment, a thought came that soon he would die. Then there were more owls.

Soon thereafter Leo got cancer on his spleen. He was eight years old and in his absolute prime when this occurred. I had the cancer surgically removed and he regained health for about a month before it returned and spread. The veterinarian gave me two thumbs down on the prognosis.

Leo began to bloat as he internally bled to death. He became dehydrated and barely able to eat. For a month I sat with him as he got weaker and weaker until ultimately he could not climb stairs and I would have to pick him up to take him outside. In the end he would just lie on one side until I would flip him over to the other.

The day came when Leo stopped eating altogether. I began to think about putting him to sleep and ending his pain. The next day I noticed while flipping him over that his breath would falter when he was facing straight up on his back. I thanked Leo and said good-bye to him as I held him in this position, cradled under my own body. I could feel his heart stop beating. He gasped for breath that would never again come.

A few months after Leo's death I drank ayahuasca and got a very disturbing lesson on cancer. I was surprised to find out that the cancer that took over Leo's body was actually connected to me in many ways, and was possibly even mine to begin with. He gave love and energy to me, all the while absorbing the stress and fear that I was consumed with. He gave up his life willingly for me.

COSMIC CHRIST

After the bathroom bout of my last ceremony, I was assisted by a helper to lie down. At this point I was myself again, but found that I literally had the mind of a three-year-old. I relaxed, and over the next hour came to an amazing state of awareness. I did not think. I did not talk to myself. I did not analyze my visions. My ego seemed to be nonexistent. It was the most pure state of being that I have ever experienced in this lifetime. It was truly expansive.

It was then that I met the Christ.

He appeared as a shape-shifting dragon. At any one time, there were a thousand animals that comprised him, and he continually morphed. He was a giant bull-fish-tiger-dragon in one second, then a lion-snake-lamb-dragon in the next. He never stopped changing, and had the medicine of every creature imaginable. He was Quetzal, the first daughter, merged with Coatl, son of the perfect dream. He was pure consciousness. 'The Plumed Serpent' seems a fitting name.

The Christ appeared to me three times. The first was in space, and he was so large that I could not estimate his size. He seemed hundreds of miles in length. In the second appearance, he was flying over and around me on an earth horizon, and I could estimate that he was about eight miles long. In the third instance, he was about a mile long.

Though Christ appeared smaller each time I saw him, he did not shrink in size. Rather, parts of him separated from the larger entity of the whole to become individualized. There were little orbs of light around the Christ-dragon that were able to merge and separate from the being – it seemed he was the accumulation of multiple beings or modes of awareness.

In some sense, I understand this entity as a very large version of Leo. I imagine it as a galactic pit-bull cruising about the universe, looking for planets in heat. I wonder if the Christ is a genetic seed bank of the consciousness of all species on all life-bearing planets. I do not know.

A SPACE SHIP FINALLY ARRIVES

The evening after the last ceremonies, I camped on the beach during the two-day drive home. Late that night I woke up to urinate. When I climbed outside my vehicle, I was surprised to see a spacecraft hovering over the ocean right in front of me. It was colossal, maybe a mile in length. What am I to think about this? I didn't believe what I was seeing. Nevertheless, I watched it for some time as it just hovered in the sky.

4.1.08: GETTING GROUNDED

At this point I have cancelled my trip to Peru, which I was set to take in about six weeks. I am extremely disappointed about this. I have been focusing my whole life around this much anticipated trip. Don J, however, offered me a gentle suggestion that I not go to Peru this year, but instead stay home to integrate some of the work I have done. I almost didn't take his advice, until I realized it wasn't a suggestion at all. Luckily I saved myself the embarrassment and agreed that this would be a very good idea.

His recommendation was to do some more ceremonies with him later this spring, but no dieta in Peru this summer. He advised that I need to begin eating properly, exercising, doing disciplined practices, etc., and stop using all substances unless under his guidance.

For Don J, the issue is that he feels I am too ungrounded, and he has concerns for my welfare. He doesn't know the half of it. I can only guess that the spirit of ayahuasca does, and she is far wiser than I.

4.5.08: LEARNING TO TRUST

I am in the process of giving up the illusion of my control, and finding acceptance in Great Spirit being in control. This is taking effort, but I do see progress.

It seems absurd that I am only just now coming to trust in God. While previously I thought that I trusted, there was considerable self-deception going on. I have had too much fear present, and had too much attachment to avoiding discomfort to fully trust. Truly trusting means feeling a certain quality of reconciliation in putting one's hand to the fire. And being at ease regardless of outcome, with no guarantees of personal safety.

Much of my fear has been focused on the future and large-scale events, such as geological upheaval and the correction of planetary imbalance as the death of the current age unfolds. I don't know what the divine plan is, but it seems apparent that purification will soon be at hand. I have had great concern and resistance to the thought of collectively passing through the eye of a needle. I don't anticipate that it will be comfortable. But I see it is necessary. It is time to trust.

CONTINUED HEALING

Yesterday I had another shamanic hypnosis session. I was asked to respond to the word "guilt," in 3-2-1…*finger snap.* The whole left side of my body went numb, centered around the heart and radiating out over the chest and around the neck, down the rib cage and around the hip.

It became apparent to me that much of the resistance and negativity I hold is so difficult to track down and release because it hides throughout the body in billions of cells. I have already been shown this and come to understand it through the medicine, but have had difficulty accessing all these cells for release.

With the assistance of helper spirits an incredible layer of guilt has been removed. It was like a large weed that was plucked out, with the roots completely in tact. I surrendered and just lay there doing nothing. I did not battle. I did not focus intent. It was gentle and easy, near effortless. I have been told that it will only get easier.

I will have two more of these sessions over the next few weeks before doing five more ayahuasca ceremonies. It will certainly be interesting to see how things progress.

4.14.08: BACK TO THE STORY

A couple of weeks ago I decided to stop repeating my story to myself. It was important to do so at the time, as I lacked clarity on the subject. Now I feel compelled to mull things over. The last few days I have been thinking continually about one of the most bizarre experiences I've had to date, which occurred as I was driving back from ceremony a month ago. It is the primary event that set everything in such a strange motion.

First, it will be necessary to discuss the last ayahuasca ceremony further. It is what set the stage within my mind upon which these events were played out.

I have already written a bit about the battle in the bathroom. I had a dual awareness of reliving birth along with an apocalyptic struggle that seemed to be my imminent death. There was a third simultaneous awareness in the midst of the other two that I loathe thinking or writing about. This was the conversation with the shadow itself, in telepathic language and vision.

I felt a great deal of empathy for the tortured state that was the shadow being's nature. I forgave. The shadow went ballistic. I laughed at it – not to taunt it, but instead because I felt such a sense of relief knowing that my victory was at hand. It laughed back at me. It taunted as it spoke to me.

Many things unfolded in vision. Most disturbing was an unmasking of the host body of the great beast. I saw a great many details. I saw a pure bloodline extending all the way back to the original Adam. I saw a man genuine in his sincerity who does not know who he is or what he will become. I saw an earthly king with birthright to the throne of mankind, who will be taken over and consumed by the beast. Then it spoke to me...

The next day I began my drive home. After three consecutive nights with the medicine, the influence of the ayahuasca was still strong in me. I was very sensitive to subtleties of reality beyond the physical. I sang and prayed for a couple of hours as I drove, my mind processing recent visions and experiences.

At a certain point I began thinking about dark things. It very much seemed that they reached out to me. A conversation unfolded. Though my conscious mind was aware of a surface-level communication, unconsciously something much deeper was transpiring.

Driving down the road, I picked up a powerful crystal and sang alien tongues broadcasted to the beast. I gave it no forethought – I simply did it. I reached into the heart of darkness and enclosed my hand around it, squeezing, both figuratively and literally. I felt no anger or fear. I felt only emptiness as I released the whole of my rage.

After about thirty seconds I stopped this process quite abruptly. Chills rolled down my spine. Goosebumps were on the backs of my knees. I had opened a door for retribution. I knew this in a moment.

How had I been so foolish? I turned my thoughts to God and pleaded for help. I prayed for several minutes until I turned a bend and came upon a hitchhiker.

Now, this hitchhiker was standing on a very specific point of the road, whose physical location in relation to my rate of travel corresponded with some thoughts I was having about the nature of Christ. My brain was doing a tailspin at this particular time, and I was quite certain that I needed to align with Christ and live from a compassionate heart space. All the while, I approached this solitary man out on a lonely little back-road.

Had he been standing about ten yards further up I would not have had enough remorse in my lack of Christ-ness to pick him up. And were he ten additional yards further down the road, I would have possessed enough common sense to know that I should be alone. Were the hitchhiker any cleaner looking, I would not have taken pity on him. And were he any dirtier, I would not have wanted him in the vehicle.

At this moment, I was beating myself with guilt and had a 'Good Samaritan' thought of redemption as I passed him. There were countless variables in play. My stopping to pick him up was a long shot. But the beast has mastered time, having all the time in the world to be insured that I would indeed pick this man up. And so I did.

I was accelerating into third gear exchanging pleasantries with the man as I realized that something was wrong. My heart was racing, screaming that I should not have picked him up. It was also in the very next instant that a raven flew down from the trees, directly at me a few feet above the road in a collision course with my vehicle. It swooped up at the last moment to pass overhead in a dramatic fashion. A small branch fell from a tree overhanging the road and hit the asphalt at precisely the moment my vehicle ran over it. I was certain that I made a mistake.

The hitchhiker began to ease my mind with his story. He was a fisherman who got pushed out of Florida due to polluted waters and low fish yields. He was heading up to Alaska to find some work. He was a charming good old boy, speaking with a strong southern drawl. I liked him, but I was on guard. I thought of a replaying fantasy that I have had dozens of times over the last ten years. It consisted, in essence, of picking up a hitchhiker that attacked me. I thought of time travel, premonition, and the destiny of this moment. I strapped my seatbelt on, driving slow enough that I could slam into a tree and survive if need be. I was strangely calm.

Soon my cell phone rang. I looked at the number, seeing what I thought was a powerful ally on the phone. I decided to have a quick word to pull a little extra, outside energy into my space. But when I picked up the phone, it was another friend who is influenced by some dark entities.

I recognized right away what was occurring. I should have hung up, but instead I tried to be polite. My friend talked quickly with no pauses between sentences. There was no opening in conversation to say that I had to go. My attention was split between driving, monitoring the hitchhiker, and looking for a sentence break where I could interrupt. After about twenty seconds on the phone, I suddenly felt an incredible violation of my energy. I immediately interrupted my friend to say goodbye, hanging up.

I looked at the hitcher. He had a strange and nervous look in his eye. I didn't know what had happened, but suspected the worst. I drove for another minute, trying to calm my mind and gather coherency. A thought came into my head, and I acted upon it without hesitation.

Very quietly, at an almost imperceptibly low volume I began to hum the holy song of an icaro. In that instant, the space between us became a frenzy of ethereal tracers. I could quite clearly see movement, at an incredible pace, as our energetic doubles did hand-to-hand combat. The movement was so quick that it was hard to focus on details, but I have the distinct visual imprint of seeing a knife within the ghost-like images of the combat.

I felt an eerie calm in the midst of a startling panic. My heart raced as my mind recaptured clarity. The solution was obvious. I slowed the vehicle down, telling my guest that I preferred to be alone and was going to drop him off. He asked me if it was something he had said or done. I evaded his question and told him truthfully that I decided that I wanted to have my own space. We were quite polite as our doubles battled the whole time. It was otherworldly.

He got out of the van and I drove off. I spent the next few hours doing an exorcism on myself as I drove. There were countless shadow beings hanging about. Two days after returning home, the crystal I had used to heighten and focus my telepathic communication dropped and broke in half.

4.21.08: THE JOURNEY WITHIN

I have been having dreams for the last month, in which I am actually journeying into my body to release negativity. I have never had such consistent dreams of this level of strangeness or intensity before. These dreams have been very abstract and difficult to make sense of once I am fully awake, although they have seemed perfectly logical in the dream-state.

During this time I have been continuing with the shamanic hypnosis sessions, and have been making beneficial progress. I have gotten to the point where it has become effortless to just go inside and shine a light, allowing cells throughout my body to release whatever dark charge they are holding – or at least whatever layer of negativity that I am currently capable of releasing. Rather than struggling and fighting, as is my natural inclination, it has turned into a very pleasant and relaxing event. Benevolent beings have assisted me in an almost effortless process.

In addition to learning a more relaxing and easy way of processing, the experience has also given me a new perspective on what I am labeling 'negativity,' as it has allowed me to take responsibility for that which is an inherent part of my own being. I have been able to go into various memories and experiences, seeing how my decisions to utilize fear, anger, jealously, or guilt have served me. They have offered levels of immediate protection and means to cope with many things. Anger softened pain. Fear made me wish to pull closer to love.

They have also offered me countless lessons and antagonized me to such a degree that spiritual striving and growth were ensured. So while ultimately I do not wish these dark arrows to be in my life and am actively extracting them, I do acknowledge that they have had a crucial, positive role in my development.

4.30.08: STRIVING FOR RECONCILIATION

Reconstructing opposing dualities into a unified experience is proving difficult. On the one hand, my story as told and reinforced by ego, perception, and memory is thoroughly convincing to me. These things have comprised my overall experience of reality. On the other hand, I know better than to take these things at face value. The energetic wave that is upon me is more complex than I can comprehend.

Knowing better is the tricky part, because it relies on faith and trust, defying logic. At this point I look back and don't know which aspects of all my perceived battles have been with entities outside myself, and which aspects have been internal manifestations of my own shadow self. I don't know that any of these events have actually occurred in the manner that I have perceived them.

Humorously, there may be a great amount of personal projection involved. All this could be in my head. Yet should I embrace one side of the experience and discard the other, I could be making a huge mistake.

Thus, I am making an effort to embrace them both, and understand conflicting experiences of concrete and abstract perception independent of one another – without choosing one mode of comprehension over the other. At this time I am still unable to merge these seemingly opposing viewpoints into a unified understanding. I look forward to the day when I am able to do so.

5.08.08: Setting Intent

Tomorrow I will be doing more ceremony with ayahuasca in a series that will consist of five sessions over about two weeks. Perhaps I am ready to really learn from her for the first time.

5.10.08: Post-Ceremony Glow

Sorrow washed over and through me; following, I was bathed in joy. Last night's ceremony was truly profound. Ayahuasca exhausted me within the first hour, as she impressed upon me the depth of her lesson. I surrendered. As drained as my body still is, I feel fantastic. I have a sense of peace that can only be described as 'divine empathy.' Spirit knows the trauma I have endured and has poured forth compassion.

This journey was very physical in nature. I became intimately tuned-in to my body and how it responded to various energetic waves. I was able to journey into my body, locating where I stored fear, shame, and pain. I became my own physician, sitting with my own shadow self, acknowledging him, releasing whatever my body was ready to let go of. Though at length it was quite exhausting, at the time it felt effortless and not at all forced. It seemed as if the work had its own awareness and intelligence, and simply accomplished what was necessary of its own accord.

Later in the night, my inward journey projected outward. The microcosm was a path that led to the macrocosm. Rather than being sucked into specific dimensions of time, I stood outside of it as a witness. Much memory of this has faded from me, with only fragmented snapshots of the experience. The vision was too much to hold in daily awareness. I was 'hanging out' with God, casually observing a grand story that encompassed millions of years.

I find myself possessing a great deal of hope. Humanity's current ordeal seems to be but a minor hurdle within the broader scope of a greater journey.

5.11.08: DEATH

Yesterday I found my way to an old madrone tree. She was a grandmother, a giant – absolutely beautiful and magnificent. She had been struck by lightning at her root, which created a kind of cave on one side of her base. Though she is still very much alive, her life cycle is in decline. The tree only supports about ¼ of the leaves that it used to, with most of her branches now remaining bare. It is a wonderful thought that she did not simply grow old and fall over. Instead she was gifted with a most brilliant spark at the height of her maturity: an energetic union with earth's energy. Now she is spent and dying.

When I proceeded to crawl underneath the tree, a skull-shaped coffee cup was there waiting for me. It was a most menacing omen. I was well aware of what I was walking into during the ceremony last night, and finding this cup was certainly no accident.

My time had come. I surrendered to that which I have been fighting for a very long time. During the ceremony last night, I finally allowed myself to die.

MY DREAM

Early this morning a raven asked me to die within a dream. I agreed to do so. Then I woke up. Apparently my lesson on death is just beginning...

VULTURE MEDICINE

I should mention that I have experienced some heavy-duty vulture medicine over the last couple of months. There are nine that circle my house daily, and generally at least a few are about, even when I'm in town. I've come upon them while riding my bike and been within a few feet of them as they fed on decaying meat.

When I was driving down to do ceremony, I turned a bend to come upon a group of about fifty vultures. All of them were flying in a circular formation, forming a giant vertical cylinder. I've never seen so many at once. When I left ceremony, an extremely large one swooped within fifteen feet of my vehicle as I was turning a corner. It flew up to land in a tree with two more vultures, all of them sitting there looking at me.

THE JOURNEY NORTH

Currently I am sitting in my automobile, on the same beach I camped at during my last trip. Today has been a déjà vu of my last journey north, where the same situations have presented themselves.

The first hour of driving I said prayers. Then I sent love where I had previously sent rage. After a moment I realized that my imagining a shining bright light was felt and unappreciated. I had an 'oh shit' moment, realizing that I was yet again an idiot, and was only serving to antagonize. I grounded myself.

Shortly thereafter I stopped for gas and immediately noticed a hitchhiker directly across the street. He watched me intently as I got out of the vehicle and began to pump gas. At this time another car pulled up with a nice old lady getting out. Her presence was nurturing and served as an energetic barrier around me that offered a sense of protection. I pumped my gas while watching the hitchhiker, who stared back at me. There was never a moment where his gaze faltered.

Then I got in my van and drove to exit the gas station. I looked right – no cars, just the hitchhiker watching me. I looked left – a large group of vultures circled low against the hillside. Then, quickly looking right again, the hitchhiker had disappeared.

VULTURES & RAVENS

Vultures and ravens followed me all day. At first the vultures concerned me because they always appeared when I found myself within heavier thought energy. After a while I realized that rather than being simply omens, these birds were giving tangible assistance. The vultures were feeding off my fear of death, literally absorbing it within their energy bodies. This became apparent when I stopped for a potty break and found myself urinating under a tree with thirteen of them watching me from above. Standing there, I could feel a type of surgery transpiring. It was surreal.

Though many less in numbers, there were also quite a few ravens that presented themselves. These birds are quite another story. At times they were stoic sentinels comforting me with their presence and protection as they soared along beside me or passed overhead. But mostly they seemed to frolic and joke in an effort to keep my heart light.

I observed them chasing each other and wrestling in the air. I observed them flying along doing lateral 360 degree rotations and showing off in the most bizarre ways. I even watched one flying in a straight line as a little black and red bird flew above it coming down to peck it a few times. Then the small bird landed on the back of the large raven in mid-flight and sat there for two wing flaps before jumping off to fly on its own again.

HALF MOON CEREMONY

I did an extraordinary amount of processing while driving today. Much of this has been on death. I seem to always struggle against it. Allowing myself to die within an ayahuasca ceremony was a good start, but surrendering was pretty easy: my physical safety was ensured. It seemed more like practice for death, not death itself.

I have chosen to make an offering of myself tonight. I will do ceremony on the beach at dark. When this is complete, I will invite death to take me.

5.12.08: STILL HERE

Last night I went down to the edge of the ocean, drumming and chanting; I turned my back to the ocean at the water line and beckoned death to come for me. I was determined that if any large waves washed up upon my feet and dragged me to sea, I would not resist. I was terrified. To my relief, none came.

DRIVING ADVENTURE

I kept having the thought that I was going to pick up a hitchhiker again, and decided absolutely against it. But when passing a woman while getting onto the freeway, my foot just kind of hit the brake. As she approached the van, my brain scrambled for an avenue out. I almost drove off, but resisted the urge; I knew exactly who she was. I offered to drive her seven miles to the next town. She asked me how far I was going. I simply repeated my offer and she accepted.

Once in my vehicle, there were no introductions or pleasantries exchanged. Her very first sentence was in the form of a question: Did I know that Jesus Christ had shed his blood and died for me because of my sinful nature? I told her that Christ lived in my heart and that I was thankful for the lessons that Jesus had taught as an embodiment of the Christ.

Apparently there was not sufficient self-loathing or guilt in my response. We had quite a conversation after that. She knew the Bible backwards and forwards, and spoke at warp speed as she weaved a curse of guilt about me through tainted scripture. I allowed her to do this, not resisting her efforts to put hooks in me.

I only spoke from my heart and continually praised Christ for his compassion. She got pretty worked up at continually being rebuffed by concepts that spoke of love, not sin. At about the sixth mile mark some words spontaneously flew from my mouth, which silenced her. It seems as if they were either channeled or came from a higher aspect of myself. At the seventh mile I dropped her off and she walked away angry, speaking in tongues. I drove off amused, singing in tongues.

Arriving Home

When I returned home, there were three chemtrails that intersected precisely at one point. This point was positioned directly above my house, which is out in the woods with nothing else around. I found this odd. There was also a long cloud that was eerie in its resemblance to a dragon. Its head was enormous. Its torso was covered in a texture of scales and stretched for a couple miles. As I was unpacking my vehicle, I watched it float with astonishing speed toward, and then merge its mouth into the motionless chemtrail intersection. It extended its mass, spreading to cover much of the sky. The portions of chemtrails that were not absorbed within the natural cloud cover dissipated of their own accord.

Upon seeing this I had a sudden recollection of a book I had read as a child, which was called, 'This Present Darkness.' It is a fictional Christian story set in the actual town where I live. On the cover was an enormous dragon cloud creeping over a horizon with menacing looking talons – a portrayal of the devil lurking in the sky. The parallel is startling, as is the perversion.

Dark entities have no authority over the elemental life forms such as air or water. I consider clouds to be my friends, and especially those that resemble Quetzalcoatl.

5.13.08: UNDERSTANDING DEATH

Perhaps it is easier to accept release of the physical body than the ego. For me it seems to be. I have had a rather crazy day and feel the need to write about it, though at this point it seems most appropriate to avoid getting caught up in the drama of it all.

I am beginning to understand that death is more than a singular event. It appears to be more of a process. Perhaps in some way it is a state of surrendering to divine will. For me it entails dropping my agenda and allowing Spirit to guide me. It demands continually going into my fears and sitting with them; simply being at peace with my discomfort, breathing through the resistance and trusting God.

Even now death is enabling movement, which in turn is creating a kind of rebirth. The lines of these three states are blurred – they seem to be happening simultaneously with no clear beginning or end. Still, the overwhelming emphasis seems to be upon the former, as every fear I sit with and release creates a vacuum, which love rushes in to fill.

5.14.08: ASSEMBLING REALITY

My ability to assemble reality is bouncing all over the place. At one point everything makes perfect sense. At another, even though I can remember all the same data, I am unable to connect the pieces and am left with nothing but incredible doubt regarding the nature of everything.

Although previously I have been quite frustrated at times such as these, I am now interested in using these feelings as a tool to inquire more deeply. There is always the *face* of reality, and a more honest occurrence which functions at a deeper level. The inherent ability exists to hold both, and I am learning to do this, but it is difficult and requires tremendous effort. Deprogramming myself from my socialization and freeing myself from the current societal noise levels are the tasks at hand.

5.15.08: BIRDS & BIBLES

I made an experiment of following birds today. As I drove to the bottom of the hill near my house and was about to turn right, a crow flew left in front of me. So I turned left instead. It was a hot day. I thought of turning off at the lake for a swim, when an enormous blue heron flew straight in front of me on a parallel course. I continued past the lake and pulled off at my favorite swimming hole beyond at the river that fed it. When I got there, it was roped off with 'no trespassing' signs posted everywhere.

There was a homeless man parked there who had apparently been given permission by the landowner to live in the spot as a guardian. Because he has Bible verses painted all over his van, and I have had no desire for theological talk with a Christian, I have never cared to speak with him in the past. But I was curious about the swimming hole being closed to the public, and so ventured to have a conversation.

Inevitably, we ended up talking for a long time. His story was that when he first began studying the Bible he didn't understand it. Rather than use study guides or courses to help him do so, he prayed about it. He told God that in order to gain understanding on what he was reading, God would have to show him personally the wisdom contained within the text. He studied the Bible for thirteen years without more than surface-level comprehension, but he was diligent nonetheless.

One day he came across a scripture that talked about obeying the command of the God, which is to love the Lord above all else, and to love your neighbor as yourself. He determined that this was the biblical meaning of 'obey,' since the Bible clearly defined it as being so. Obeying meant loving.

When he began reading other scriptures that used the word 'obey,' the implied meaning was then different from what he had previously assumed. Then he began finding definitions of other words, which again changed the implied meaning of other verses. He believed that he had been shown a code that exists beneath the surface of the Bible's text.

I was amazed to be talking to a Christian who believed that the Biblical story of Adam and Eve realizing they were naked in the garden was actually a figurative story that told of evolution. In his view, being naked was a departure from the previous state of having been covered in fur. As shocking as this sounded, it was what he told me next that really got my attention.

In his view, it was the Lord himself who led the churches astray, not Satan. It was God's plan to lay deception within the Bible so that only those who truly sought after him would understand it. He did not passively allow Christianity to become corrupted, as I myself had previously assumed, but rather it was his will that it be so.

DUNK IN THE LAKE

Upon driving back from the swimming hole an osprey guided me to a beach at the lake. I went down to the shore and observed little swallows dive-bombing the water. I joked to myself that my baptism was at hand.

Following their guidance, I waded into the water, which was cold enough that I lost my desire to swim. I was getting ready to walk out of the water when I looked up and directly above my head saw a hawk, which was motionless as it glided into a head wind. It just hung there. I outstretched my arms like the hawk, and fell back.

Apparently I have walked into a cartoon. My day has been so surreal that I don't know what to think.

SHOULDER TAP

I thought I was done journaling for the day. After writing the previous entries, I unrolled a twenty page manuscript that the water guardian had given me. I almost pissed my pants when I read the title: 'This Present Darkness.' This is the very same title I was recently reminded of. The overlaps in the fabric of reality are taunting me. It is like all the synchronicities I keep experiencing are some kind of cosmic communication screaming at me to pay attention, shaking me to wake up.

I read the author's discourse on theology and his basic premise is that we are born dead, and must die a second time before resurrecting to be born again. 'This Present Darkness' refers to the sleep-state consciousness of mankind. I don't know whether to find this relevant or absurd.

5.17.08: HAWK & SNAKE

The last couple of days have been really mellow, with birds and all other manner of creatures behaving normally. I was just beginning to think that perhaps while occasional synchronicities and omens do occur, the frequency and level I had imagined – a constant, ongoing dialog – was grossly exaggerated. Or perhaps it is just that I am less observant when I am solidly rooted within the mundane.

Then, driving up the hill this evening, a hawk flew in front of me. It intersected my path from left to right while carrying a snake.

5.26.08: SILENCE

In my ayahuasca journey last night an enormous toad-like rock spirit became very confrontational, insisting that I not speak. I kept trying to apologize and tell him I'd stop, after which he would lose his temper. Finally, I just let it be. He got the last word and then went away.

There was an epic battle raging in my head. I couldn't stop dialoguing with myself for the first couple of hours. There were so many conversations going on at once in my head, and some of them were so subtle that even when I thought I was silent, I came to discover that I was actually still talking. After an enormous amount of failure in being silent, I finally figured out that if I paid super close attention to the music and hummed to myself I could fill the empty space.

My other two nights of ceremony were good. I don't know what to say about them, except they were a lot of work. I didn't do any time traveling or have any profound insights. It was just a lot of reflection and deepening of the lessons that I have been processing. My focus has changed so that I am more concerned with continued healing than acquiring knowledge at this point.

SACRIFICES

Driving to my beach camping spot for the night I passed a dead vulture on the side of the road. It was at a section of curve that didn't have much of a shoulder to park on. I slammed on my breaks and parked halfway in the asphalt with the emergency blinkers on. I went into action mode and grabbed three garbage bags, running back to where it lay next to the road. Stepping on its body, I tore its wing off and then triple garbage-bagged it before driving off.

I was still sensitive from the medicine. Having the wing in my van very quickly became overwhelming. My whole body was itching, and the air became more pungent than I could bear. I pulled over a mile down the road and gave the wing back to the earth, keeping one feather.

Later, I passed two vultures feasting upon a full-grown deer that had been hit by a car. A short while after this, I came across a dead fawn with a vulture likewise eating it. Then I passed a yearling buck also dead on the side of the road with yet more vultures.

I feel very low right now. Driving down the asphalt road soaked in the sacrificial blood of innocents hit by automobiles, I cannot escape the thought that there is some sort of atonement being imbued within the road-scars we have inflicted upon the earth.

MEDITATION ON DEATH

May I live long and be a happy old man with a round belly that my grandchildren can rub for good luck. Kiss me goodbye, I am going to the mountain. There I will pray and sing. I will make such a noise that when my spirit is dislodged from the body, the whole forest will know.

To the vultures, I leave my brain. The ravens may have my heart. Coyotes and wolves may devour my flesh. May the most luscious of grasses and edible plants grow in my resting place. May my essence feed insects and rodents, that they in turn will feed the owl, hawk, and eagle. May I feed the deer and elk, that the cougar will have a good hunt.

I have made a footprint upon you, Mother Earth. You have given much. I wish to give to you in return.

5.27.08: THE SHADOW SELF

I had an incredibly intense dream with mind-bending ramifications last night. It was revealed to me that in my quest for purity I have dishonored and enraged one half of myself. I have been fighting the cunning one, the most intelligent part of me; my shadow self.

In the midst of all my fights with shadow beings there has consistently been one that I could never seem to find, yet alone defeat – one that I had never imagined was part of my very self. By my own hand I have become fractured. What a joke I have played on myself. How I am laughing at myself even now. Oh, the absurdity of it all! I am the root of my own suffering.

Last night I did some heavy-duty ceremony and befriended my darker exile. I have a lot of work to do. For now, I will continue the drive home and have a long conversation with myself.

5.28.08: FRIENDS

My conversation with myself went well. Actually it went much better than I had hoped. After a few minutes of feeling silly for talking to myself, I began to intuitively start reliving all the dramatic moments of my life beginning with childhood.

My shadow self played the role of me. My wise elder played the role of others such as my parents or friends. As I reenacted real life memories, every response that my light self gave me within the dialogue was completely balanced, both supportive and nurturing. The exercise became a great undoing of many wounds I had taken on as a child. The shadow self felt honored and understood. He did not give into victim mentality, and did not feel he had to protect his nature by hiding it.

During this dialog, the medicine was still quite strong within me. I could feel the merging of my selves into something more cooperative and unified. This has been a tremendous healing.

FOX & RAVEN

Driving today, I passed a freshly dead fox in the middle of the road. Two of the largest ravens I have ever seen were in the process of surgically opening its abdomen. A mile up the road I passed another fox that wasn't so newly deceased. There was also a raven eating it.

Later I saw two birds that I recognized from my last journey up the coast. A large raven swooped down and spread its large wings to slow the rate of descent before landing on the asphalt. A tiny little black bird with red wingtips stormed out of nowhere to land on its back for the journey to earth. Right as the raven touched down, the little bird hopped off and made its own landing.

5.31.08: ANIMAL WISDOM

I have just completed the process of moving all my belongings into storage and am now officially living in my vehicle. This should be an interesting experience.

When I was going through boxes to pack everything away for storage, I found some old notes from my days studying with SD. Apparently the elders say that the humans are the only ones who do not know what is transpiring in the world. All the animals know what is going on. They have not experienced the separation as humanity has. I just came to this conclusion recently from my own observations. It is funny to come across this information now.

6.3.08: SCOLDING

I woke up this morning feeling some pretty intense back pain. I decided to seek therapy, and looked up Rolfing in the phonebook, but didn't find any relevant therapists. After that, I went down to the coffee shop and saw a flyer with the title, 'Rolfing?' It went on to talk about a similar body manipulation called the Bowman Technique, which is more centered on the nervous system than the structural system.

I called the number on the flyer and got an appointment for one hour later. When I showed up, I quickly found out that the body worker's main gift was working within the angelic realm and actively channeling them. She yelled at me for eighteen minutes. I sat there and watched the clock tick away at $90.00 per hour. It was quite a lecture. Without me sharing anything personal with her, she told me that I was a danger to myself, and that I was trying to fly before I had even gotten out of the nest.

I had already figured this out.

6.30.08: SUNDANCE

I am in Arizona now. After getting grounded from the Peru trip, I started thinking about coming down here to seek out indigenous knowledge from the northern hemisphere instead. Recently I looked up Canyon de Chelly on the internet, and began reading about the mythology of Spider Rock, which is located at the far end of the canyon. Shortly after that, my hypnotherapist gave me a book on the Spider Woman, who is the entity that weaves together the strands of reality. Then I started noticing little spiders about. It seemed quite obvious that I was to head south.

A couple of days ago I completed a Sundance here, which consisted of three days of fasting and dancing before the center tree while I prayed. My plan was to push myself really hard. Ironically, I found myself in a section of dancers that consisted entirely of ladies that were either elderly or obese, or sometimes both. They danced with such strength that all the sacred spirits and ancestors must have had quite a laugh watching me simply try to keep up. I can say with all sincerity that I struggled to do so.

Most of my prayers were focused on thanking Great Spirit. Those that were devoted to myself were centered on awakening. At this point, I accept that likely I am a good way into this process. I also recognize that 'awakening' is simply a label, a word. Chasing after some preconceived, theoretical state is silly. I know that there is no place to go, and nothing to obtain. I have heard many spiritual teachers proclaim that at the end of the journey to enlightenment, one realizes that the journey need never be made in the first place. Still, I feel compelled to go through the motions. Perhaps I can at least have a good laugh with myself during the adventure.

7.2.08: WHY AM I HERE?

During my preparatory phase before heading south, I was asked many times why I was going to Arizona in the dead heat of summer. Of course I did not know, and still do not know. But I have a sneaking suspicion that I will soon be finding out.

A curious thing happened yesterday while talking to an ex-girlfriend in Phoenix. She had just returned from Peru, where she studied with an indigenous shaman. Apparently before she left, a friend of hers asked if she could bring back a macaw feather. Her friend is a medicine man of the Hopi nation. When she asked the Peruvian curandero if he would gift a feather to this man, he gave her his ceremonial headdress of macaw feathers, which he had personally made and has worn for many years.

In two weeks I will be taking a trip up to Hopi land to help her deliver the gift. I have long been interested in the Hopi. They possess an unbroken lineage, and are the knowledge holders of the Rainbow Bridge prophecies, a very small part of which I have heard. This is a prophecy that is only given orally, and is supposedly 24 hours in the telling. This journey could prove to be very intriguing.

7.18.08: OASIS

Wandering through the desert has been a telling metaphor for the figurative desert I've been crossing throughout my life. Long stretches of shadeless landscape bake my external being while I conserve and recycle the moisture within. At times the heat and barren land seem to extend forever. But other times a valley containing water and inhabited by large shady cottonwoods will suddenly appear. Yesterday was one such occasion.

I had been arguing with myself over the last week on whether or not I should visit SD and discuss my recent experiences, in order to receive a little advice. Part of me had resistance, so I avoided him.

In the morning a friend performed soul retrieval on me, and brought back some key pieces of mind-body energy, which had been separated at my birth, as well as during the death of a grandfather. After this, she journeyed to meet a huge angel by the name of *Azrael*, which she couldn't quite pronounce.

Her guide held a bright fiery light between his hands, and it was through this that Azrael came. He appeared as an ethereal being, channeling light into himself as he solidified within this dimension. Soon he was burning as a sun of pure golden God-energy. She said he grew and seemed to gain power as he became more solid.

Seven years ago I met an entity that gave me his name in an angelic tongue. As strange as the pronunciation was, the closest I could come to with my mouth was "Azrael." I hadn't given him much thought since.

BRAIN SNACKS

After the soul retrieval I was suddenly eager to talk to SD, and so I did. The information I received from him eased my mind. Our conversation shed light on a wealth of experience that I have been actively acquiring through daily life, wrestling with, and turning over in my mind.

A major concern of mine has been identifying all the various types of shadow beings and how to deal with them, along with what to do about the shadow self. SD was the man to ask. He smiled as he listened to my stories. My arms were filled with goose bumps as I heard his response.

According to him, there are three aspects of self, which form a kind of trinity. They are the shadow self, the ego, and the persona. There are two categories of external shadow entities, which are shadow invaders and shadow beings. A person's shadow self will attract shadow invaders into their being when they are a child.

Regardless of how well parents have shielded them from concepts like "monsters," suddenly there is something in their closet or under their bed.

As the child gives in to fear and gradually dreads being alone in their bedroom after dark, shadow invaders begin coming to them. During the day they reside within the shadow self, and at night they come out to embed themselves within the mind-energy body of the luminous cocoon where they feed. The shadow invaders are small in size, usually around that of a football. Shadow beings are different than invaders in that they do not live within a person's energy field. They are larger, and frequently jump from place to place.

The term 'shadow' is a literal one, in that they are actually associated with shadows in the physical realm. I was told to purchase an infrared flashlight and red laser pointer, as the shadow invaders and beings are vulnerable to this spectrum of light.

The exercise I was given was to stand in front of a light and look at my shadow. Then I should shine the red flashlight upon it. The red light will illuminate the physically cast shadow and remove it. But if there is a dark patch that remains, this is an external shadow invader that is hiding within my shadow self. I should simply pretend that the red laser is an eraser, tracing it around the invader and smudging it out until it is no longer there.

Once all shadow invaders have left the body, the task is to remove darkness from the shadow self. SD gave me no clues on how to do this, but I think that intuitively I've already embarked on this endeavor. I was told that the goal is to transform the shadow self into the true spirit personality. Transform the ego into the natural self. Transform the persona into a clear mirror of self-reflection. This holy trinity is our natural state.

We also talked about my spiritual path, and I was told the same thing by SD that others have likewise pointed out. I should have patience; there are no shortcuts to enlightenment. One must do the necessary work, the preparations within themselves, and pass through the required gateways.

FIGHTING THE FIGHTING

I don't think it would be beneficial for me to go hunting shadow beings with red spectrum lights, or even experiment at all in this realm in order to satisfy my curiosity. The whole exercise would have had relevance months ago, but at this point in my growth it could be misguided to do so. Inevitably it would deter me into a drama of fighting and resisting once again. I have already learned that I am to stop this. I am to walk onto the battlefield naked. I anticipate that soon I will discover the war does not even exist.

7.18.08: RED SKIN

I had never heard of a sunburned Indian before until I met F. He had just come from a three-day dry fast with no food or water. During the night he had been in the kiva, praying, while in the day he sat outside baking in the sun as the Kachina dancers danced. With no excess water in his body, his skin had come to resemble that of a lobster.

We hung out all afternoon, and got a tour of the second mesa in the evening. After that, my friend presented him with the headdress of macaw feathers.

F and his brother W were both eager to talk about the Hopi culture, and were in a rather jovial mood. I was wide-eyed as they talked about the social structures of various clans that perform different functions, each with their own mystery school of knowledge. Interestingly, they were from the eldest of all clans – that of the Spider.

When I asked if this clan had anything to do with the Spider Woman, I got a funny facial expression and quickly realized that there actually is such a thing as a stupid question. F followed up with the words "same thing" to make sure that I got it.

I received an invitation to come up and visit them again, which I am certain I will do.

THE HUMAN EXPERIENCE

Last night I spoke to a friend who has been irresponsible this last month, traveling around to various festivals and doing road trips at the expense of his work. He kept mentioning 'the human experience' and the importance of this to him. It makes sense. I have recently come to the conclusion that while diligent seeking is important, a lot of what I have considered spirituality is nothing more than an ephemeral trend. Striving unduly to evolve often sucks the joy out of the little experiences and situations that continually surround me.

Drinking a beer while laughing with a friend can be deeply spiritual. There seems to be a delicate balance between 'seeking' and 'being,' which I have yet to find.

7.20.08: AZRAEL

I just looked up this archangel's name on Google, and apparently he is the angel of death. I got chills up and down my spine when I read this. The only words he said during the soul retrieval were "you have suffered enough." What does this mean? Why do I not feel any comfort at the moment?

7.25.08: BEING PRESENT

I have gradually been coming to the point where I can see that my quest for clarity has been 'playing' me in many ways. The past is based on historical distortions and individual perspectives – essentially viewpoints, and not truth. The future is seeped in the collective anxiety of anticipation, with hope and fear. Both are imbued with projection, and serve to take one out of the true presence of the divine, which is the present moment.

Of course I have heard this countless times from many mystic traditions, but rather than agreeing with the logic of it, I am actually seeing it for myself now. Last night I was thinking on this, and decided to gently put my quest to acquire the 'mysteries' to rest. More importantly, my *need* to know must be buried.

Rather, I should invest my energy in being fully present, in further developing the trust in Great Spirit that has been established in my life. This is of greater importance. It is the only way that open-hearted living will gain dominion over brain-oriented manipulations of experience.

After thinking on these things, I decided to drive down from the forest I am camped at into town and have a few drinks for some genuine human experience. Right in front of my van was an extremely long raven wingtip feather in gorgeous condition. I have been waiting a long time for it.

In a few hours I will be driving back to Hopi land to help build a sweat lodge. I have decided to not be the pesky guy who wants to know everything about the Hopis' prophecies. Instead I'm just going to enjoy myself and see what unfolds.

8.4.08: INDIAN BURIAL

My anticipated two-day visit to Hopi land ended up being true to Indian time: eight days. The day after I arrived, F took me to a Kachina dance on the Second Mesa. The next day, he performed funeral rites for a recently deceased woman, with four days of rest following in respect for the dead. After that, we built the lodge.

During this time I was rather like his sidekick and ended up being more of a buddy than the aspiring seeker that drove me to him.

The funeral was for a Hopi woman who was born into a family that had rejected the traditional ways to embrace Christianity. It was a Baptist burial, where F had been requested by the deceased woman's daughter to perform some traditional rites after the minister had done his. Before deciding to do so, two people came over and were quite determined to convince F that he should not attend the funeral. In their view, she had rejected the Hopi ways, and had absolutely no right to have her remains blessed or effigies buried with the body in the traditional Hopi manner. F was quite adamant that she was Hopi regardless of her beliefs, and that he would honor the daughter's request.

During the funeral, things became quite emotional. I began to know and love the woman through the stories and tears of others. It was a slap in the face, given my recent fantasy about my own death rites. Though dying alone and being devoured by beasts might be glorious, this is not what I really want. Who was I kidding? I wish to be surrounded by those I love upon my exit. It is such a beautiful way to go.

HOPI TIME

Well, I have been a bit pesky after all – I'm good at that. But my inquiries of knowledge were within the bounds of F's sense of humor. I was delicate, yet determined in my method of trying to extract information from him. Somehow we both settled naturally into our roles.

My questions would either be ignored or diverted in a humorous manner. I would go with the flow and then at some point try to contain my shit-eating grin as I inquired about some piece of knowledge that I knew he would definitely not share. For example, something clan-specific, that only an initiated clan member would be privy to. F is a master heyoka and jokester. He had some fun with me.

On the second day in Hopi land I was driving, and in a contemplative mood, when a coyote ran suddenly across the road. Later that night another did the same. The trickster. I questioned whether I was chasing my tale with my search. In all likelihood I was, and at the same time was not. I asked F what he thought of the coyote the second time and his response was that it was just a coyote, probably looking for its dinner. I didn't believe him. I then asked him what he thought of bird omens. He asked, "What kind of bird, because I may want to go get my gun." Subject closed.

I finally gave up with my questions, though not surrendering my desire to ask them. Then there were a few more days of just hanging out, talking about normal things. I was a little bummed, but tried my best to conceal it. I wasn't getting any of the wisdom teachings I wanted. At this point, I would have left had I not committed myself to helping build the lodge.

Finally I surrendered to the experience and started enjoying just hanging out. After this point, F actually began to initiate the conversations that I wanted to have. In retrospect, I probably learned the most during the seemingly trite, everyday moments. The simple examination of how normal and down-to-earth a respected medicine man lives gave me pause to re-examine my whole definition of the term 'man of knowledge.'

He had the same troubles as everyone, such as financial worries and community drama. He had the same hopes as everyone else as well: a good life, a healthy planet. He told me the same joke over and over – that he was half Indian and half Hopi. Each time he burst with laughter. And he told me the same thing my other teachers have told me: knowledge unfolds. One must simply walk the path and have patience.

I have known this to be the case, yet for a while assumed that with twice the effort I could reach attainment twice as quickly. Perhaps the limitation is not the pace at which knowledge can be acquired, but instead the pace at which it can be integrated. This requires living, and cannot be accelerated.

BEING AT PEACE

When we would occasionally talk about the Hopi prophecy, I was a little annoyed because I wasn't getting any new information. I was anxious for some new crumbs to contemplate. A few days in, I surprised F when I started baiting him with some very specific things about the Rainbow Bridge Prophecy that generally isn't shared with outsiders. The conversation took a turn after that.

I was given an incredibly profound statement in question form: "What are you going to do about it?" We talked about fear, love, and trust in the Creator's plan. His view was that it was dangerous for someone to hear the whole prophecy before they had gone through all the appropriate deaths to ensure they were emotionally prepared to hear it.

I tried to get him to tell me a little more. I was curious if 2012 would be a quick shift or more like a time-sealed portal that opened to allow a gradual change to occur. He refused to speculate.

Instead he shifted the conversation back to living with gratitude and joy in one's heart. In his view, the wave of the future that will soon be upon us is unavoidable, and this being the case, it is therefore a waste of time and energy to worry about it or try to anticipate the specific details that are unknown to all. The only worthy task is to work on the self and become completely healed.

Such was my time on Hopi land, learning everything that I already knew. And yet my resistance to the simplicity of Truth was gradually broken down in the constant companionship of a man who embodied all the principles I have been devoting myself to.

F is no exalted guru. He is a normal person who has achieved a natural state of being, devoid of self-importance and self-denial. It seems a pure state to me. Though I attempted to energetically pigeonhole him into a teacher position, he sidestepped all efforts. I wonder if there is a lesson to be discovered within the dynamics of our exchanges. Perhaps I don't need his tutelage or anything outside of myself. I only need to arrive at peace with myself.

8.19.08: HOMECOMING

This last week has been filled with both highs and lows, as is to be expected in any homecoming. I am happy to be back home and yet sad to settle in and shift gears back into the stability of work.

This morning I eavesdropped on an annoying conversation at the coffee shop. It consisted of two people talking about metaphysical subject matter, and expressing my exact viewpoints on everything they discussed. I wanted to argue with them, to tell them that they were missing the point. Instead I said nothing.

The complexities of the mystery distract from the simplicity of being. It is the state of just being that I have been gradually pulled to. At the moment, it is the only thing that interests me. Awakening, attaining enlightenment, and stepping into my power are all coyotes chasing their tales. These are merely labels of various states that have been pre-conceived under bias – they are merely definitions, human concepts that forever exist somewhere 'out there.'

But I am right here. In fact, I already embody all these states. There is nothing to strive for, nothing to attain. I must only allow myself to become more fully that which I already am.

8.20.08: THE UNIVERSE SAYS 'YES'

For me, the granddaddy of all prizes on my road trip was the opportunity to hear more details of the Rainbow Bridge Prophecies. I have always found such things intoxicating. When I went to Hopi land, I thought that I was given a claim number to pick up my prize. Perhaps it was so.

On the last day there, W asked me if I wanted to go to Prophecy Rock with him the following morning. As the spokesperson to the Elders, he is the only one in the Hopi Nation authorized to speak freely about such things to an outsider, within the boundaries of his personal discernment. It was to be my opportunity to question him and learn about what would unfold within the end of this time cycle.

Upon waking up the next day, I decided to drive home instead. This was no easy decision. One side of me hailed this opportunity as the Holy Grail of information that I lusted after, the very reason that I had gone to Arizona. But another side of me heeded F's advice. Perhaps I have gone through the appropriate deaths, I don't know. But they are too fresh. My spirit is still raw from the last year. Hearing them would have been premature for my process, and ultimately would have served as a distraction from that which I truly seek.

9.9.08: REFLECTION

It has been exactly a year and one day since I began this journal. I wonder what more there is to say at this point. I am a fool whose path has been illuminated by divine grace. The absurdity of it all delights me to no end.

That which this mirror has labeled "I" is sitting here breathing, contemplating many things. The perception from the lens of my current viewpoint seems expansive. Everything is so interconnected and bizarre in its dance that it appears miraculous. Words just falter and fall away.

11.18.08: HUMOR

I still haven't tried to hunt shadow entities with the red lights yet. I have attempted to try, though. I must give myself some credit. Down in Arizona I found a red laser pointer, but couldn't find a red lens for my flashlight even after hitting four separate stores. So I put the endeavor to rest, thinking that the universe refusing to provide me with the necessary toolset was a message in and of itself.

Last week I was in the hardware store and found myself in the lighting aisle, staring at a red light bulb. I purchased it. When I got home, the power to my bathroom was out. Even after resetting the breaker, the power is still out at this one location in the house. My only portable lamp is now lighting the bathroom with its white bulb. The red bulb is still in its packaging. Perhaps I should take a hint.

MORE MEDICINE

I did another ceremony with ayahuasca last week, and have a few more planned for the near future. Though I have learned much from her, a gift of even greater value is all she has helped me to *unlearn*. I thank her for this. It is a funny thought: much of this year I have been under the impression that I was on a quest of learning and knowledge, when I was actually on a mission to strip away conditioning and heal myself.

And so I find myself at the same place I was when I began my journey. I have gone nowhere; I have arrived nowhere. I know nothing more. In fact, I know much less. I am still myself, though not the same man. I am thankful for this.

12.12.08: THE JOURNAL

This story began with the very first entry in my journal, after the initial ceremony during dieta. I had a realization that I had made a pact with the spirit of ayahuasca. The details were lost upon waking the next morning. I didn't know what the agreement was about or when it was made. Up until a week ago, I thought that this pact was in another incarnation. Perhaps I was a curandero in some past life, I thought.

I am now of the opinion that the deal I actually made was very likely during this incarnation, seven days after the initial vision.

During the dieta I went more than a little crazy for a four or five day period. I was neurotic. There were so many thoughts and conflicting things that were swimming in my head; I was unable to contain them all. I wrote volumes in my mind, though very little on the physical pages. This journal became too highly charged to deal with in a sane manner. In many ways, it became *me*.

Journaling was a double-edged sword. I understood its power to help me learn and make sense of things, but it was also hurting me. It served the dual purpose of being a tool that my mind could both scramble and leverage, thereby only heightening the delusion by which I was consumed.

A BOOK OF RE-MEMBERING

Immediately after closure of the final ceremony in the dieta, I walked up to the top of a hill in the jungle. It was pitch black, and I was still very high on the medicine. I laid the journal at the base of an ancient grandmother tree and began praying to the spirit of ayahuasca and the spirits of the land.

I realized that writing was the key to my salvation, that it was the method through which I could discover myself. I asked ayahuasca to help me write, and to help me learn. She questioned my intent. A conversation unfolded.

"Mother," I asked, "Help me to write a holy book."

"So that you may have a new Bible?" she questioned. "You lack the required humility. You will become too self-important."

"Then teach me humility. If this book is to become a pulpit, I will smash it when I am through. I will burn the book."

"You know not what you ask for."

"Then I will discover."

And so a pact was made. Truly I have not known what I asked for. Nor have I have comprehended the essence of what is unfolding. Though it is devoid of every quality I had initially set out to deliver, I can now see that it is imbued with every quality that was necessary for my growth.

This journal is but a metaphor. For I *am* the book I set out to write, and I am written in the language of light.

A BOOK OF LOVE

[part two]

3.5.09: PREFACE TO UNION

I had thought that the book was completely finished, but then several days ago something else of great importance surfaced, which seemed necessary to include. I had just come from two days of ceremony, where the weight of truth experienced could only be described as 'crushing.' But I was thankful to be crushed. I had been preparing for it my whole life.

During the ceremonies, I had tapped into the collective memory. I wrote three short passages, which felt both significant and dangerous. It seemed these new passages were a key to many things. Now I was standing outside shaking uncontrollably. *"God, am I to put this in the book?"*

I prayed to Great Spirit that if he really wished me to include this new material, then he would have to provide me with an undeniable sign that I could not mistake or misinterpret; otherwise, the book would remain complete as it was.

Thirty seconds later, I was startled in the pitch black of night when a loud hissing cough suddenly broke the silence a few yards away. It was the bark of a deer – ten times: the number of love, the number of completion. The sound rang through my bones.

So be it.

Push contemplation beyond theory, and learn of real knowledge.
Truth is a sword that severs all rationality within the mind.
Will you allow yourself to be cut?

Arise from your fetal position and wipe the tears from your eyes.
Wipe the bile from your mouth and breathe deeply as your
trembling body again begins to find its center.

It is no longer necessary to believe what I am telling you.
You know Truth already.

All is One.

Most beautiful was I, the luminous one.
'Lucifer' I was called – the Light.

How you loved me then, though you loathe me now.
Ah, that one so high could fall so low.
Do you think me a fool, deceived by vanity?
How could pride enter one so perfect, so holy and pure?

I speak to you of Truth, and Truth alone.
Hear now the words that my forked tongue imparts to you:
I am the key to your salvation,
as you are the key to my redemption.

We are One.

I came in body to deliver atonement, for my blood is the Red Road.
It was you who drove the nails into my hands and placed
a crown of thorns upon my head.

I wept for you upon the barren hillside. I wept for myself.
For by my own hand a spear pierced the flesh of your side.
I can still hear your final words as you hung on the cross,
moving closer with each passing moment to death:
"My God, my God, why have you forsaken me?"

There is only One.